THE NOBEL PRIZE

THE

the story of ALFRED NOBEL

MICHAEL WOREK

NOBEL PRIZE

and the most famous prize in the world

FIREFLY BOOKS

Alfred Nobel (1833–1896), scientist, inventor, poet, businessman and chemist, left most of his huge fortune to establish the Nobel Prizes — for Chemistry, Physics, Medicine, Literature and Peace.

for Karen

A Firefly Book

Published by Firefly Books Ltd. 2010

The publisher gratefully acknowledges the financial support for our publishing program by the Government of Canada through the Canada Book Fund as administered by the Department of Canadian Heritage.

First printing

Library and Archives Canada Cataloguing in Publication

Worek, Michael
    The Nobel Prize : the story of Alfred Nobel and the most famous prize in the world / Michael Worek.
Includes index.
ISBN-13: 978-1-55407-711-3   ISBN-10: 1-55407-711-7
1. Nobel Prizes--History. 2. Nobel, Alfred Bernhard, 1833-1896. I. Title.
AS911.N9W66 2010   001.4'4   C2010-901868-0

Published in the United States by
Firefly Books (U.S.) Inc.
P.O. Box 1338, Ellicott Station
Buffalo, New York 14205

Published in Canada by
Firefly Books Ltd.
66 Leek Crescent
Richmond Hill, Ontario L4B 1H1

Publisher Cataloging-in-Publication Data (U.S.)

Worek, Michael.
    The Nobel Prize : the story of Alfred Nobel and the most famous prize in the world / Michael Worek.
[ ] p. : photos. ; cm.
Includes index.
Summary: The fascinating story of how a few instructions in Nobel's Will created the philanthropic organization that holds a unique position in the modern world.
ISBN-13: 978-1-55407-711-3   ISBN-10: 1-55407-711-7
1. Nobel, Alfred Bernhard, 1833-1896. 2. Nobel Prizes – History. 3. Philanthropists -- Sweden – Biography.
4. Chemical engineers -- Sweden -- Biography. I. Title.
001.4/4 [B] dc22   AS911.N9W6745 2010

Cover and interior design: opushouse.ca
Formatting: opushouse.ca

Printed in Canada

Contents

Introduction

Individuals and institutions that receive a Nobel Prize are never called "winners" because there is no contest or competition of any kind that they have "won." Those who are selected to receive the most famous award in the world are called laureates, and to be a Nobel Prize laureate is to be recognized everywhere as a person who has made an outstanding contribution in his or her field.

Nobel Prize laureates have been deeply involved in the history and culture of the 20th century and have been instrumental in shaping the world as we know it today. Since 1901, the original Nobel Prizes have been awarded in five separate categories — Peace, Medicine, Literature, Chemistry and Physics.

In 1968 the Royal Bank of Sweden (Sveriges Riksbank) established a new Nobel Prize category in honor of its 300th anniversary and provided an endowment to fund a prize in Economics. Known officially as the Sveriges Riksbank Prize in Economic Sciences in Memory of Alfred Nobel, it is awarded to an individual who has made an outstanding contribution to the science of economics.

The directors of the Nobel Foundation later decided not to permit any further new prizes in other areas, so the five prizes established by Alfred Nobel, plus the prize in Economic Sciences, are likely to remain the only Nobel Prizes to be awarded in the future.

Not only does the Nobel Prize bring honor and recognition around the world, it also gives the Nobel laureate a cash award of more than $1,000,000 US. The prize money comes from the estate of Alfred Nobel, whose foresight and concern for the welfare of future generations motivated him to establish the prizes and to leave his vast fortune to provide the money necessary to make the awards for over a century.

The Life of Alfred Nobel

Alfred Nobel was born in Stockholm, Sweden, in 1833. His father, Immanuel Nobel, was an architect and inventor who built bridges and buildings throughout Stockholm. His mother, Andriette Ahlsell, came from a wealthy family and was a descendant of Olof Rudbeck, one of the most famous scientists in Swedish history.

In 1842 Immanuel moved his family to St. Petersburg, Russia, where he had opened a machine shop to build weapons for the Russian army. He designed a naval mine to protect the harbor of St. Petersburg, then the capital of Russia. These mines prevented the British Navy from getting close enough to shell the city during the Crimean War (1853–1856).

Alfred received a private education at home from university professors. He read widely and spoke and wrote Swedish, English, German, Russian and French. He loved chemistry, which became the basis of his experiments, his discoveries and his fortune, but he also enjoyed literature and wrote poetry. This complex man was a scientist, inventor, successful businessman and a poet.

As a young man, his father sent him abroad to study. In Paris he worked with famous chemists including Ascanio Sobrero who had invented nitroglycerine a few years earlier. After traveling around Europe and a trip to the United States, he returned to Russia to work in his father's factory.

In 1859 the business in St. Petersburg went bankrupt and Immanuel and two of his sons, Alfred and Emil, returned to Stockholm. Two other brothers, Robert and Ludvig, remained in St. Petersburg and later made their own fortune by developing the oil industry in the southern part of Russia.

Back in Sweden, Alfred began working with his father, but soon began his own experiments with the explosive nitroglycerine that was then being widely used to blast through rock in the construction of railways and canals. In 1863 he received his first patent for a detonator to be used with nitroglycerine, an extremely dangerous liquid that had to be handled with great care. In 1864 an accident at Nobel's factory caused an explosion that destroyed the factory and killed several workers including Alfred's younger brother Emil. This tragedy did not discourage him though, and he quickly established other factories to manufacture nitroglycerine.

In 1867 Nobel received a patent for his invention of dynamite. He had mixed nitroglycerine and silica together to turn the dangerous liquid nitroglycerine into a safe paste that would not explode until detonated. And then, to detonate the dynamite, he invented a blasting cap. A fuse was lit at one end and the dynamite would explode when the flame reached the blasting cap. The result was tremendous explosive force with very little risk of accidental explosion.

One major advantage of dynamite was that it could be formed in the shape of a cylinder and inserted into the holes that were commonly drilled into rock during mining and excavating. Nobel's invention came just at the moment that construction projects for cities, subways, railways, canals and tunnels were being undertaken all over the world, and the demand for his invention quickly made him famous and wealthy.

By 1864, Alfred Nobel had established a factory in Stockholm and a factory in Germany, opened a factory in the United States in 1866, and then one in France in 1870. He eventually established over 90 different factories in 20 countries around the world. Nobel's abilities as a businessman enabled him to profit from the manufacture and sale of his inventions.

Nobel traveled constantly between his factories and considered himself a citizen of the world, maintaining homes in Sweden, Germany, France and Italy. He never married, suffered from ill health all his life, and his constant work and traveling left him little time for making friends. Then, exhausted by his travels and business responsibilities, he died in 1896 in Italy at the age of 63.

The combination of brilliant inventor and astute businessman is extremely rare, and Nobel was one of the first to create a truly multinational corporation as we know them today. As well as explosives, Nobel worked on the development of synthetic rubber and artificial silk, and made advances in electrochemistry, optics, biology and physiology. In 1887 he developed ballistite, known as smokeless gunpowder, which was adopted by military forces around the world. At the time of his death, he held 355 patents. Few men have accomplished so much in either business or science and fewer still in both.

His decision to give his fortune to fund the Nobel Prize awards ensured that his name and accomplishments would always be remembered.

The contents of his will, which was handwritten and witnessed by four friends in the Swedish-Norwegian Club in Paris in 1895, were a great surprise, and he seems not to have discussed his plans for the prizes with anyone. After leaving amounts of money for his immediate family and friends, Nobel's will provides only this short summary of how he wanted the Nobel Prizes to work:

The whole of my remaining realizable estate shall be dealt with in the following way: the capital, invested in safe securities by my executors, shall constitute a fund, the interest on which shall be annually distributed in the form of prizes to those who, during the preceding year, shall have conferred the greatest benefit on mankind. The said interest shall be divided into five equal parts, which shall be apportioned as follows: one part to the person who shall have made the most important discovery or invention within the field of physics; one part to the person who shall have made the most important chemical discovery or improvement; one part to the person who shall have made the most important discovery within the domain of physiology or medicine; one part to the person who shall have produced in the field of literature the most outstanding work in an ideal direction; and one part to the person who shall have done the most or the best work for fraternity between nations, for the abolition or reduction of standing armies and for the holding and promotion of peace congresses. The prizes for physics and chemistry shall be awarded by the Swedish Academy of Sciences; that for physiological or medical work by the Karolinska Institute in Stockholm; that for literature by the Academy in Stockholm, and that for champions of peace by a committee of five persons to be elected by the Norwegian Storting. It is my express wish that in awarding the prizes no consideration

whatever shall be given to the nationality of the candidates, but that the most
worthy shall receive the prize, whether he be a Scandinavian or not.

At the time of his death, Nobel's fortune was estimated to be about 31
million Swedish kronor. His immediate relatives wanted to contest the
will and receive a greater share of his fortune, and there were many legal
and administrative problems to overcome before everyone was satisfied. In
addition, Nobel had not asked the various institutions that he charged with
awarding prizes if they would be willing to take on this responsibility, and he
made no provision to pay them for their work. There were no details in the
will about how the laureates were to be chosen or about how the money was
to be invested and managed.

Nobel appointed two young engineers with whom he had worked, Ragnar
Sohlman and Rudolf Lilljequist, as executors of his will. They were responsible
for creating the Nobel Foundation and making Alfred Nobel's dream a reality.
In 1901, only five years after his death, the first Nobel Prize awards were made
on December 10, the anniversary of his death.

Nobel was a complex and brilliant man who, had he not been the one
to establish the prize, and had he lived for a few more years, might well have
been nominated for his achievements in science. Yet, because his most famous
and profitable inventions were explosives, there has long been a feeling that
Nobel established the Peace Prize to atone for the harm done by the use of his
discoveries in war.

Public perception of Nobel as a man who had grown rich through the
suffering and death of those killed in war was common. As early as 1888, a
French newspaper called him a "merchant of death." Albert Einstein, a man
who was himself often directly identified with the development of the atomic
bomb, referred specifically to Nobel in speaking about the moral responsibility
scientists have for the use to which their inventions are put: "Alfred Nobel
invented an explosive more powerful than any then known — an exceedingly
effective means of destruction. To atone for this 'accomplishment' and to

relieve his conscience, he instituted his award for the promotion of peace."

The idea that the inventor of so much destructive power was attempting to balance the scale for good when he established the Nobel Prizes (although without foundation in Nobel's own words) seems to be commonly accepted. However, Nobel certainly believed in the power of science to work for the betterment of mankind as well as its destruction.

Bertha von Suttner, a well known peace activist and, for a short time, Nobel's personal secretary, arranged for many international peace conferences and wrote a book entitled *Lay Down Your Arms* that argued for disarmament. In a letter to her in 1891, Nobel expressed the hope that his invention would result in world peace, not more war: "Perhaps my factories will put an end to war sooner than your congresses; on the day that two army corps can mutually annihilate each other in a second, all civilized nations will surely recoil with horror and disband their troops." In 1905 Bertha von Suttner received the Nobel Peace Prize for her work for world peace and disarmament.

The Nobel Prize

Each year since 1901, the Nobel Prize committees have met to review the names of people nominated to receive a Nobel Prize. Because the Nobel Prize is an international award, names are submitted from countries around the world and many of the laureates in physics, chemistry and medicine are little known outside the scientific community. Those who are awarded the prize for literature and peace are often more famous, but even many of these are little known outside their field before they receive the award.

Nobel Prizes are awarded for life and cannot be revoked no matter what the laureate does after receiving the prize. Laureates receive a gold medal, a certificate and a cash award. The money for each award in 2009 amounted to 10 million Swedish kronor, about $1,400,000 in United States currency.

Laureates are announced in October each year. The award ceremonies for physics, chemistry, medicine, literature and economics are held in Stockholm, Sweden, on December 10. The awards are presented by the King of Sweden. The Nobel Peace Prize is presented in Oslo, Norway, by the Chairman of the Norwegian Nobel Committee with the King of Norway present at the ceremony.

The Nobel Prize ceremonies at which the prizes are presented have been suspended occasionally — from 1914 to 1918 and again from 1939 to 1943, when it would have been almost impossible to travel to Norway and Sweden because the world was at war. In 1940, 1941 and 1942 no prize awards were made. In 1924 the festivities were cancelled because neither of the only two laureates named that year could attend.

Before 1974 the statutes that govern the Nobel Foundation allowed a deceased person to receive a prize so long as the person was alive and had been nominated before February 1 in the year the prize was awarded. Under this clause, the prize for Literature in 1931 went to Erik Karlfeldt who died on April 8, and the prize for Peace in 1961 went to Dag Hammarskjöld, who died on September 18, 1961. Since 1974, however, the prize may only be given to a deceased person if the person dies after the prize awards have been announced, usually in October, but before the actual date of the award presentation on December 10.

Between 1901 and 2009, the six Nobel Prizes have been awarded 537 times. Since many prizes have been awarded to two or three individuals and the prize has occasionally been presented to the same individual or organization more than once, a total of 802 individuals and 20 organizations have received the prize. 765 prizes have been awarded to men and 41 prizes to women. Prizes can only be awarded to individuals except for the Peace Prize, which may also be awarded to institutions.

The Nobel Prizes have been awarded as follows:

The Nobel Prize in Physics – 186 individuals have shared the 103 awards in Physics. John Bardeen received the Physics prize twice, in 1956 and 1972.

The Nobel Prize in Chemistry – 156 individuals have shared the 101 awards in Chemistry. Frederick Sanger received the Chemistry prize twice, in 1958 and 1980.

The Nobel Prize in Medicine – 195 individuals have shared the 100 awards in Medicine. No individual has been honored more than once.

The Nobel Prize in Literature – 106 individuals have shared the 102 awards in Literature. No individual has been honored more than once.

The Nobel Peace Prize – 120 individuals and organizations have shared the 90 awards for Peace. The awards have been made to individuals 97 times and to organizations 23 times. No individual has been honored more than once. However, the International Committee of the Red Cross was awarded the prize in 1917, 1944 and 1963, and The Office of the United Nations High Commissioner for Refugees was awarded the prize in 1954 and 1981.

The Nobel Prize in Economic Sciences – 64 individuals have shared the 41 awards in Economics. No individual has been honored more than once.

Individuals who receive the Nobel Prize in Physics, Chemistry and Economics are chosen by the Royal Swedish Academy of Sciences. The Nobel Assembly of the Karolinska Institute selects the recipients of the Nobel Prize in Medicine. The recipient of the Nobel Prize in Literature is selected by the Swedish Academy. The Nobel Peace Prize laureate is selected by a committee of five persons chosen by the Norwegian Parliament.

The Royal Swedish Academy of Sciences was founded in 1739 and is the leading scientific institution in Sweden. The Karolinska Institute was founded in 1818 and is the leading medical institution in Sweden. The Swedish Academy was founded in 1786 by King Gustaf III to promote the development of Swedish language and literature. There is no special reason why the Norwegian Parliament was given the honor of selecting the Peace Prize laureate while the remainder of the Prizes are awarded by institutions in Sweden. At the time of Nobel's death in 1896, Sweden and Norway were united as one country and remained so until 1905.

Alfred Nobel's will does not restrict the number of people who may share an award, but in 1968 the Foundation adopted a resolution that stated, "In no case may a prize be divided between more than three persons." Teams of scientists working together often make advancements in science and the number of shared prizes is highest in Physics and Medicine where more shared prizes than single awards have been made.

In Literature, the awards have been overwhelmingly given to individual authors. The four times the Literature prize has been shared by two authors are Frédéric Mistral and José Echegaray (1904); Karl Gjellerup and Henrik Pontoppidan (1917); Shmuel Agnon and Nelly Sachs (1966); and Eyvind Johnson and Harry Martinson (1974). The single occasion in which three shared the Peace Prize occurred in 1994 when Yasser Arafat, Shimon Peres and Yitzhak Rabin received the prize.

Prize Category	Number of Prizes Awarded to		
	1 Laureate	2 Laureates (shared)	3 Laureates (shared)
Physics	47	28	28
Chemistry	62	22	17
Medicine	37	31	32
Literature	98	4	0
Peace	61	28	1
Economics	22	15	4
Total	327	128	82

The Nobel Prize has been declined twice. Jean-Paul Sartre was awarded the Nobel Prize in Literature in 1964 but declined to accept it on the grounds that he had always declined all honors and awards made to him. In 1973 the Nobel Peace Prize was awarded to Le Duc Tho and Henry Kissinger for their part in negotiating a ceasefire agreement in Vietnam. Kissinger accepted the award, but Le Duc Tho refused the honor because peace still had not come to Vietnam.

Four laureates have been forced by their governments to refuse the prize: Germany's Richard Kuhn for Chemistry in 1938, Adolf Butenandt for Chemistry in 1939 and Gerhard Domagk, for Medicine in 1939, when Adolf Hitler refused to let them accept the awards. Then in 1958, Boris Pasternak received the Nobel Prize in Literature. He initially accepted the prize, but the government of the Soviet Union later forced him to refuse it.

The youngest person to receive a Nobel Prize was Lawrence Bragg who received the prize in Physics in 1915 when he was only 25 years old. He shared the prize with his father for their work using X-rays to analyze the structure of crystals. The oldest person to receive a Nobel Prize was Leonid Hurwicz who received the prize in Economics in 2007 at the age of 90. Only one person has received an unshared Nobel Prize in two different categories. Linus Pauling received the Nobel Prize in Chemistry in 1954 and the Nobel Peace Prize in 1962.

Nobel Prizes have been awarded to more than one member of a family on several occasions. Marie Curie, the first woman to receive a Nobel prize, and her husband Pierre Curie jointly received the prize for Physics in 1903 and then, in 1911, Mme Curie received her second, this time for Chemistry. Their daughter Irène Joliot-Curie and her husband Frédéric Joliot together received the prize for Chemistry in 1935.

Gerty Cori and her husband Carl Cori were awarded the prize in 1947 for Medicine; Alva Myrdal, for Peace in 1982 and her husband Gunnar Myrdal in 1974 for Economics; William Bragg and his son Lawrence for Physics in 1915; Niels Bohr in 1922 for Physics and his son Aage N. Bohr in 1975, also for Physics; Hans von Euler-Chelpin, 1929 for Chemistry and his son Ulf von Euler in 1970 for Medicine; Arthur Kornberg in 1959 for Medicine and son Roger D. Kornberg in 2006 for Chemistry; Manne Siegbahn and son Kai M. Siegbahn, both for Physics, in 1924 and 1981 respectively; J.J. Thomson for Physics in 1906 and son George Paget Thomson also for Physics in 1937. Brothers Jan Tinbergen and Nikolaas Tinbergen both received the prize, Jan in 1969 for Economics and Nikolaas for Medicine in 1973.

Because few women were permitted or encouraged to attend university and take prominent roles in business and government in the early years of the 20th century, the majority of Nobel Prize laureates have been men. Between 1901 and 1950 only 11 women received a Nobel Prize. However, between 1951 and 2009, 29 women have been awarded the prize, almost three times as many as in the previous 50 years. A total of 41 Nobel Prizes have been awarded to women. The award has been given to women twice in Physics, four times in Chemistry, ten times in Medicine, twelve times in Literature, twelve times in Peace, and once in Economics.

Each year, between 100 and 250 people are nominated for each award. The selection committees may choose not to award a prize in any year if they do not feel there is a nominee worthy of the prize.

Alfred Nobel's intention in creating the awards was not just to reward and recognize individuals for their past achievements, but also to enable them to devote the time needed to make further advances in their field without worrying about money.

In 1901 the cash award for the first prizes amounted to 150,000 kronor, which was approximately 20 times the average salary paid to a university professor. As the century progressed, much of the income from the Nobel Foundation's investments was used to pay taxes. In 1923, the year in which the value of the Nobel Prize monetary award reached its lowest point, the Nobel Foundation was the largest single taxpayer in Stockholm.

In 1946 the Foundation was granted an exemption from paying tax in Sweden, and in 1953 the Foundation was granted an exemption from paying tax in the United States. These exemptions allowed the Nobel Foundation to increase the amount of the prize money paid out each year.

In 1953 the investment rules were also changed to allow the Foundation to invest in stocks and real estate instead of just high quality government bonds — the "safe security" specified in Alfred Nobel's will. The freedom from paying taxes and the ability to invest in more profitable areas has allowed the Foundation to restore the real value of the prize, after inflation, to the 1901 levels. In 2009 the cash award was 10 million Swedish kronor.

The Nobel Prize is administered by the Nobel Foundation based in Stockholm. The Foundation's responsibility is to invest the fortune as stipulated in Alfred Nobel's will, and to make the interest earned available as prize money each year. The Foundation is also responsible for arranging the presentation ceremony held each year. The Foundation itself does not receive nominations for the prizes or select laureates.

A board of directors that consists of seven members and two deputies controls the Foundation. All members of the board must be Swedish or Norwegian citizens. The institutions that select the recipients of the Nobel Prizes (the Swedish Academy of Sciences, the Karolinska Institute, the Swedish Academy and the Norwegian Parliament) also elect the members of the board who invest the money and control the administration of the Nobel Foundation. This means that the selection of the laureates is completely independent of the Nobel Foundation and those charged with investing the money have no say in the selection of those who receive the awards.

The entire Nobel Prize organization is private and not associated or funded by any government agency anywhere in the world. The only role played by the Swedish government in the Nobel Foundation is to appoint one of the Foundation's auditors who oversee the investment of the money that makes the awards possible.

The nomination and selection process that results in the selection of each year's awards is a very formal process. For example, the Norwegian Nobel Committee, the body responsible for making the Nobel Peace Prize award, is composed of five members appointed by the Norwegian Parliament.

In September every year the Norwegian Committee sends out letters to individuals qualified to nominate candidates for the Peace Prize. These include members of national assemblies, governments and international courts of law; university chancellors; professors of social science, history, philosophy, law and theology; leaders of peace research institutes and institutes of foreign affairs; previous Nobel Peace Prize laureates; board members of organizations that have received the Nobel Peace Prize; present and past members of the Norwegian Nobel Committee; and former advisers of the Norwegian Nobel Institute.

Nominations must be postmarked no later than February 1 of the following year. In recent years, the Committee has received close to 200 different nominations for the Nobel Peace Prize. During February and March, the Committee assesses each candidate and prepares a short list of names for consideration. Advisers who are specially selected for their knowledge of the candidates review the short list. The advisers do not directly evaluate nominations nor give explicit recommendations.

At the beginning of October, the Nobel Committee chooses the Nobel Peace Prize laureates through a majority vote. The decision is final and without appeal. The name or names of the Nobel Peace Prize laureate(s) are then announced. The Nobel Peace Prize Award ceremony takes place on December 10 in Oslo, Norway, where the laureates receive their Nobel Prize.

The fame and prestige of the Nobel Prize has made it a model for other organizations that wish to establish an international prize. In 1985 the Science and Technology Foundation of Japan established the Japan Prize. Their first award of 50 million yen went to the Nobel Foundation "in recognition of the role the Nobel Foundation has played since 1901 in promoting science and international understanding." In the same year, the Kyoto Prize was established and awarded 45 million yen to the Nobel Foundation in recognition of its work in promoting science and technology. These prestigious awards directly acknowledged the impact the Nobel Prize has had on the advancement of science around the world.

The Nobel Prize

The advancement in science in the last century has been so rapid and so profound that it is now almost impossible to image the world as it existed when Alfred Nobel established the prize that bears his name. At Nobel's death, steam engines and horses powered the world. Communication was by letter and medical care was in its infancy. In little more than 100 years, science has taken us to the moon, revealed the secrets of the atom, photographed the distant galaxies, discovered the genetic key to who we are and eliminated to a great extent the most dread diseases of history — tuberculosis, malaria, smallpox, diphtheria, polio, and yellow fever.

No less revolutionary has been the advance in communication that has put us instantly and continuously in touch with each other anywhere on the planet. Cell phones, radio, television, the computer and the Internet have literally annihilated the barriers of time and distance that once kept us apart.

But new discoveries have proven to be dangerous as well as beneficial. Atomic

Science

power and atomic bombs exist side by side, promising unlimited energy on the one hand and unlimited destruction on the other. Insecticides like DDT can kill insects that spread disease but, at the same time, kill the birds that feed on the insects.

Nobel was a brilliant scientist himself, and so it is not surprising that there are three separate prizes for science — Physics, Chemistry and Medicine — in his will. And the advances in these sciences that have made possible the world we know today are chronicled in the Nobel Prizes that have been awarded since his death.

Like the escaped contents of Pandora's box, scientific discoveries once made can never be hidden away again. Our moral and ethical sense as human beings, our sense of the sacredness of human life, a respect for justice, human rights and diversity must grow and mature at a pace equal to our increasing scientific knowledge, lest we misuse the power we've been given. It was this hope that underscored Alfred Nobel's desire to reward those scientists who had "conferred the greatest benefit on mankind."

Science

In 1902 Ronald Ross, a surgeon in the Indian Army, received the second Nobel prize to be awarded in Medicine for his discovery that the virus that caused malaria developed inside the body of mosquitoes. Previous to this discovery, it was known that malaria was spread by mosquitoes, but not how the disease developed. Ross's work opened the way to further research on how one of the deadliest diseases on Earth was spread from victim to victim and led to the development of an effective vaccine.

Between 1903 and 1935 Marie Curie, her husband Pierre Curie, their daughter Irène Joliot-Curie and their son-in-law Frédéric Joliot all received a Nobel prize. No other family has produced so many laureates and few have made such fundamental discoveries in science. Marie and Pierre Curie and Henri Becquerel were honored with the Nobel Prize in Physics for the discovery of radioactivity in 1903. In 1911 Marie again received the prize, this time for Chemistry, for her discovery of two previously unknown chemical elements — radium and polonium. Irène Joliot-Curie and her husband Frédéric were honored with

the Nobel Prize in Chemistry in 1935 for their work in synthesizing new radioactive elements.

The Nobel Prize in Chemistry for 1908 was awarded to Ernest Rutherford for research into the structure of the atom and his pioneering work in creating a model of the atom itself. The Nobel Prize Committee referred to him as the man who "to such an

Marie and Pierre Curie shared the 1903 Nobel Prize in Physics with Henri Becquerel for their work in radiation.

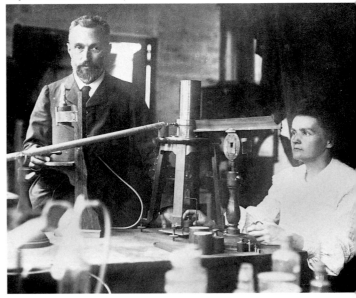

extraordinary degree wrung their secrets from the atoms."

In 1909 the Nobel Prize in Physics was awarded to Guglielmo Marconi and Karl Braun for their work in sending electrical signals over great distances without the use of telegraph wires. This development was called "wireless telegraphy" and was especially important in communication with ships at sea. It was used in 1912 by the *Titanic* to call for help after it had hit an iceberg.

The prize in Physics was awarded to Max Planck in 1918 for his mathematical formula for the law of general radiation. As an indication of the significance of his work, the Nobel Committee commented, "it will be a long time before the treasures will be exhausted which have been unearthed as a result of Planck's genius."

In 1921 the Nobel Prize in Physics was awarded to Albert Einstein, specifically for his work on the quantum theory established by Planck. Einstein established basic laws for energy and the frequency of light waves.

The next year, 1922, the Physics prize went to Niels Bohr who was able to show that the orbit of the electrons determined the chemical properties of the atom. This discovery was considered so significant that it was described by the Committee as a step along the road of acquiring "fundamental truths" in science.

The Physics prize was awarded to Arthur Compton and Charles Wilson in 1927 for their work with X-rays. Material subjected

In 1909 the Physics prize went to Guglielmo Marconi and Karl Braun for the development of wireless telegraphy.

Enrico Fermi received the Nobel Prize in Physics in 1938 for his research in nuclear physics and the development of the quantum theory.

to X-rays emitted radiation according to Einstein's photoelectric laws. Compton's experiments, a major step forward in understanding the nature of X-rays, found that scattered radiation consists of two types — one the same wavelength as the source of the original X-ray and another with a longer wavelength.

In 1935 the Physics prize went to James Chadwick for his discovery of the neutron. The neutron is an atomic particle without any electric charge that has the same weight as the nucleus of an atom of hydrogen. This discovery was another major step along the road to fully understanding the structure of atoms.

The Nobel Prize in Physics in 1945 was awarded to Wolfgang Pauli for his discovery of a new law of nature, the exclusion principle, which determines the order and patterns that govern the arrangement of electrons that surround the nucleus of an atom. The exclusion principle also governs the arrangement of the neutrons and protons in the atom.

In 1951 the prize for Physics was shared between John Cockcroft and Ernest Walton for their work in bombarding the nucleus of an atom with charged particles. They proved that a hydrogen nucleus that is projected into a lithium nucleus breaks into two helium nuclei that are emitted with great energy in opposite directions. For the first time, this change had happened under human control. This work with particle acceleration was described by the Committee as having "introduced a totally new epoch in nuclear research."

Frederick Banting and John Macleod shared the Nobel Prize for Medicine in 1923 for their discovery of insulin. Their very first experiments on dogs resulted in a dramatic drop in blood sugar levels, and insulin was soon used successfully on humans. Insulin is not a cure for diabetes, but it reduces the severity of the disease and allows the diabetic to lead a more normal life.

Karl Landsteiner received the Nobel Prize in Medicine in 1930 for the discovery of the four types of human blood: A, B, AB and O. Previous to his discovery, blood transfusions were often unsuccessful. Understanding blood types made possible advances in other areas of medicine.

The Nobel Prize in Medicine for 1945 was awarded to Alexander Fleming, Ernst Chain and Howard Florey for the discovery of penicillin. Penicillin is one of the most

Albert Einstein received the Physics prize in 1921 for his work on the quantum theory.

The 1922 prize for Physics went to Niels Bohr for discovering the chemical properties of the atom.

effective drugs in the fight against the bacteria responsible for such diseases as pneumonia, meningitis, diphtheria, anthrax and gangrene.

In 1948 the Nobel Prize in Medicine was awarded to Paul Müller for his development of DDT as an extremely effective insecticide. Müller was looking for a way to control insects that harm crops when he realized that his discovery could also be used to control insects that spread disease among humans. In 1943 there was an outbreak of typhus in Italy. Over a million people were treated with DDT to kill the lice that spread the disease and the outbreak was stopped, saving thousands of lives. DDT later proved so effective that it was used to kill mosquitoes that spread malaria, and it became one of the most widely used insecticides in the world. At the time, the terrible long-term effects of DDT in the environment were as yet unknown, and it was described as "practically non-toxic to humans."

The Nobel Prize for Medicine was awarded to Max Theiler in 1951 for his development of an inoculation against yellow fever. Yellow fever was responsible for the deaths of millions of people in Africa, the Caribbean and South America. During the Spanish-American War, Dr. Walter Reed found that yellow fever was caused by a virus, and that the disease was spread by mosquitoes. Theiler discovered that the virus could be transmitted to white mice and thus could be studied in the laboratory under controlled conditions. Working with mice, he developed a vaccine against the virus that caused yellow fever, which saved millions of lives and opened many tropical areas of the world to settlement.

In 1952 the Nobel Prize in Medicine went to Selman Waksman for his work that led to the discovery of streptomycin, the first effective remedy against tuberculosis. Tuberculosis had been one of the most dreaded diseases throughout history. Streptomycin is an antibiotic that stops the growth of the tuberculosis bacteria and, in some cases, destroys it. As a result of Waksman's discovery, tuberculosis has been almost eradicated in most of the world. In presenting the award, Waksman was described by the Committee as "one of the greatest benefactors to mankind."

Linus Pauling was awarded the Nobel Prize in two different categories. A brilliant chemist, Pauling received the Nobel Prize in Chemistry in 1954 for discovering the nature of the chemical bonds that govern how atoms join together to form different compounds.

Wolfgang Pauli discovered a new law of nature regarding atoms, for which he received the 1945 Physics prize.

Frederick Banting was awarded the 1923 prize for Medicine (shared with John Macleod) for the discovery of insulin that allowed diabetics to lead a more normal life.

In 1962 Pauling was again awarded a Nobel Prize, this time for Peace to recognize his efforts from 1946 to 1962 opposing further development and testing of the hydrogen bomb. During these years Pauling lectured and wrote extensively about the dangers of atomic testing. He was especially concerned with atmospheric testing of nuclear weapons and warned that the radiation released could seriously harm life everywhere on the planet. Pauling also argued that the spread of nuclear weapons to many nations would greatly increase the chance they would someday be used in war.

In awarding him the Peace Prize, the Nobel Committee noted that Pauling's opposition to the testing and spread of nuclear weapons had contributed greatly to the test ban treaties that were finally signed in 1963. He was also commended for his belief that scientists bear an ethical responsibility for the use of their discoveries.

Frederick Sanger was awarded the Nobel

Prize in Chemistry in 1958 for his discovery of how the 51 amino acids of the insulin molecule are linked together in two strands. It took 15 years of work for Sanger to map the structure of insulin. In presenting the award, the Committee noted, "It was Alfred Nobel's intention that his prizes should not only be considered as awards for achievements done, but that they should also serve as encouragement for future work." In 1980 Sanger was awarded his second Nobel Prize in Chemistry, this time for his work on understanding and mapping the structure of DNA. He shared this prize with Paul Berg and

For his work leading to the discovery of the first effective remedy for tuberculosis, Selman Waksman received the 1952 Nobel Prize in Medicine.

Alexander Fleming was awarded the 1945 Nobel Prize in Medicine (shared with Ernst Chain and Howard Florey) for the discovery of penicillin.

Walter Gilbert.

In 1962 the Nobel Prize in Medicine was awarded to Francis Crick, James Watson and Maurice Wilkins for their discovery of the three-dimensional structure of DNA. Their work showed how DNA is composed of a sugar and a phosphate combined with three or four types of nitrogen bases, and how these basic building blocks of DNA are coupled together. The Nobel Committee noted that their work was "of utmost importance for our understanding of one of the most vital biological processes."

The Nobel Prize in Physics was awarded to John Bardeen, William Shockley and Walter Brattain in 1956 for their work in developing the transistor. John Bardeen received the prize in Physics again in 1972 along with Leon Cooper and J. Robert Schrieffer for the theory of superconductivity that states that metals chilled to a very low temperature have almost no resistance to electricity passing through them.

Willard Libby was awarded the Nobel Prize in Chemistry in 1960 for his development of the carbon 14 method of radioactive dating. Radioactive substances break down at a consistent rate over time. Carbon 14, a radioactive isotope found only in material that was once living, takes 5,600 years to break down one-half its atoms to nitrogen. Since the breakdown begins at the time the organism dies, scientists can determine how long it has been since death by checking how far along the decomposition process has gone. Using Libby's method, scientists can now determine the age of many archaeological and biological specimens and thus help us understand the past. Because it is easy to understand how carbon 14 dating works, and because it tells us more about human history, the Committee noted, "seldom has a single discovery generated such wide public interest."

The 1966 Nobel Prize in Medicine was awarded to Peyton Rous and Charles Huggins for their work showing that viruses are involved in the growth and multiplication of cancer cells. This discovery led to the development of hormone therapy as an effective treatment in the battle to control the spread of cancer.

The Nobel Prize in Physics was awarded to Dennis Gabor in 1971 for his work in developing the three-dimensional image technology of the holograph. This discovery works by using the light from a laser to determine the position of each object under observation to a fraction of a light wavelength and has allowed enormous advances in science and medical diagnosis.

In 1974 the Nobel Prize in Medicine was

Linus Pauling received the Nobel Prize twice: first in Chemistry (1954) and then for Peace (1962). His opposition to the testing and spread of nuclear weapons contributed to the signing of the 1963 test ban treaties.

William Shockley shared the prize for Physics in 1956 with John Bardeen and Walter Brattain for their work in developing the transistor.

The 1983 Nobel Prize in Medicine went to Barbara McClintock for her pioneering research in the field of genetics (long before the discovery of DNA).

shared between Albert Claude, Christian de Duve and George Palade for their work in the development of cell biology. Because cells are so small, even with an electron microscope, it is impossible to see inside them. A million cells can fit on the head of a pin, and the components inside each cell number another million times as small as the cell itself. De Duve pioneered a method of preparing cells for the electron microscope so that each individual component could be seen and studied.

In 1979 the Nobel Prize in Medicine was awarded to Allan Cormack and Godfrey Hounsfield for their work on developing computer assisted tomography, commonly known as the CAT scan. Unlike X-rays, which present only a flat, two-dimensional image,

a CAT scan replaces X-ray film with a crystal and presents a three-dimensional image generated by a computer. The accuracy and precision of the image allows doctors to use radiation treatment to kill cancer cells with great precision.

The Nobel Prize in Chemistry was awarded to Paul Berg, Walter Gilbert and Fredrick Sanger in 1980 for their work in understanding the relationship between the chemical structure and biological function of the genetic material of the body. Part of Berg's research involved combining DNA from different species, research that is fundamental in understanding the way in which hereditary traits are passed from generation to generation.

In 1983 the Nobel Prize for Medicine

Mario Molina (shared with Paul Crutzen and F. Sherwood Rowland) was awarded the prize in Chemistry in 1995 for the crucial study of the ozone layer, and the danger to it posed by nitrogen oxides and CFC gases.

was awarded to Barbara McClintock for her pioneering research on the influence of mobile genetic elements in the chromosomes that determine the pigmentation patterns of maize. Her work began more than 30 years before she received the Nobel Prize and long before the discovery of DNA. The Nobel Committee noted that she carried on her work alone and that "she was far ahead of the developments in other fields of genetics."

In 1987 the Nobel Prize in Medicine was awarded to Susumu Tonegawa for his discoveries showing the genetic background and structure of our immune system. Antibodies in the immune system prevent infection in the body. Antibodies are produced by a special kind of white blood cell called lymphocytes, and each antibody is capable of producing its own unique response to infection. The total immune system response capability is immense with many billion possible variations.

The Nobel Prize in Physics was awarded

to Norman Ramsey, Hans Dehmelt and Wolfgang Paul in 1989 for their pioneering work using an ion trap to isolate and study a single atom. Their work has been used in the development of the atomic clock, a measurement based on the time it takes for the cesium atom to make a certain number of oscillations. The atomic clock has an accuracy of one-thousandth of a second in 300 years. Such precise measurements of time have verified Einstein's general theory of relativity and allows us to measure continental drift.

The Nobel Prize in Medicine for 1993 was awarded to Richard Roberts and Phillip Sharp for their work in genetics. Working independently, both men discovered that genes in higher organisms were composed of different segments rather than being a single complete strand of DNA as had been previously assumed. The discovery of the "split genes" led to the understanding that these segments combine in different ways to create new genes and to pass on different genetic characteristics. This fundamental work has opened the way for much modern genetic research.

Mario Molina, Paul Crutzen and F. Sherwood Rowland were awarded the Nobel Prize in Chemistry in 1995 for their study of the ozone layer, an atmospheric band that surrounds Earth from about 10 to 30 miles (15 to 50 km) above the surface. In

In 2002, the prize in Medicine was given to John Sulston (shared with Sydney Brenner and Robert Horvitz) for work in increasing the understanding of genetics.

Jack Kilby received the 2000 Nobel Prize in Physics for work in developing information technology systems (shared with Zhores Alferov and Herbert Kroemer). Kilby's work on the "chip" led to the development of modern computers.

this layer the chemical ozone exists in very low density, but is extremely important since ozone is able to absorb most of the sun's ultraviolet rays before they reach Earth's surface. Without ozone, the ultraviolet radiation of the sun would make life impossible on land. Their research pointed out the dangers to the ozone layer. The flight of supersonic aircraft can release nitrogen oxides, which can decompose ozone, directly into the ozone layer. The CFC gases used in spray cans and refrigerators can also damage the ozone layer.

The discovery of the "ozone hole" over the Antarctic raised new concerns about the speed of change in the atmosphere and the need for immediate action to reduce all greenhouse gases and global warming. In presenting the award, the Nobel Committee noted that this research has "contributed to our salvation from a global environmental problem that could have catastrophic consequences."

The Nobel Prize in Physics for 2000 was awarded to Zhores Alferov, Herbert Kroemer and Jack Kilby for their discoveries that contributed to the development of our modern information technology systems. Together, these three laureates were pioneers in the design and development of rapid transistors, laser diodes and integrated circuits. Kilby's work on the integrated circuit, the chip, was fundamental to the development of modern computers. Alferov and Kroemer developed the transistors that are the basis of modern radio and cell phone communications and the laser diodes that drive the flow of data over the fiber-optic cables of the Internet.

The Nobel Prize in Medicine was awarded to Sydney Brenner, John Sulston and Robert Horvitz in 2002 for their pioneering work on how cells are genetically programmed to die and be replaced in an orderly fashion. Their work was a fundamental step forward in our understanding of the genetic system.

In 2003 the Nobel Prize in Medicine was awarded to Paul Lauterbur and Peter Mansfield for their development of magnetic resonance imaging (MRI) that is able to create an extremely accurate image for

Elizabeth Blackburn, left, and Carol Greider shared the 2009 prize for Medicine (shared with Jack Szostak) for research on how chromosomes function in cell division.

Zhores Alferov received the Nobel Prize in Physics for 2000 (shared with Herbert Kroemer and Jack Kilby) for work leading to the development of information technology systems.

research and medical diagnostic use.

The Nobel Prize in Medicine for 2006 was awarded to Andrew Fire and Craig Mello for their work in genetics. Their research has shown how the body controls the flow of genetic information in the DNA through the use of double-stranded RNA. The discovery of how the RNA works to control the transmission of DNA genetic coding has led to major advances in the understanding of high blood cholesterol, cardiovascular diseases and cancer.

In 2009 the Nobel Prize in Medicine was awarded to Elizabeth Blackburn, Carol Greider and Jack Szostak for their work in discovering how certain chromosomes found at the end of DNA functioned during cell division. Their work was described by the Committee as having "provided fundamental insights into human biology and disease mechanisms."

Thomas Steitz was awarded the Chemistry 2009 prize (shared with Ada Yonath and Venkatraman Ramakrishnan) for "studies of the structure and function of the ribosome."

The Nobel Prize

Alfred Nobel's intention, as expressed in his will, was that the prize for Literature would be awarded for "the most outstanding work in an ideal direction." By this he meant the award should go to a work that deals with important themes and issues that are of universal importance.

The announcement of the awards of the Nobel Prizes in Physics, Chemistry and Medicine always focuses on the significance of the discoveries and advancements, so that non-scientists can understand why the award was made. The Nobel Peace Prize, too, is awarded for accomplishments in areas with which the general public is familiar.

The reason why one literary work is deemed worthy of a Nobel prize and another is not, however, is often not clear. The appreciation of literature, like music and the visual arts, is subjective — different people like and value different things — so there is no easy answer to "why" an author has been chosen as any particular year's laureate. The Nobel Committee often points out that the author has managed to express ideas or feelings that were intensely felt by many, but

Literature

previously unexpressed in words. Literature, at its best, gives voice to emotions and ideas shared by all of us, whether those emotions are of joy, fear or sadness.

Most Nobel Prize awards in Literature are given for fiction, either novels or poetry. Only occasionally, as in the case of Winston Churchill's *A History of the English Speaking Peoples*, has the prize been awarded for nonfiction.

Literature, unlike music and the visual arts, depends on the audience's ability to read the language in which the work was written. We may understand the ideas and the characters in a great novel originally written in a language we don't understand, but the true greatness of any work is at least partially lost in translation. In poetry, the words chosen are the very essence of the art.

The Nobel Prizes in Literature recognize authors from around the world who, over the past century, have created memorable works which entertain and enlighten us, as well as create the symbols and myths that link us to the past and provide a glimpse into our common future.

Literature

In 1907 the Nobel Prize for Literature was awarded to Rudyard Kipling, an English author who captured the essence of the British Empire at its height. Kipling was born in India, educated for a time in England, and then returned to India as a journalist. His fascination with India's culture and people provided the material for his greatest literary works. It was said of Kipling that his great works, especially *Barrack Room Ballads*, *The Jungle Book* and *Kim*, "have brought India nearer home to the English nation than has the construction of the Suez Canal."

The dramatist and social critic George Bernard Shaw received the Nobel Prize in Literature in 1925. Shaw's plays were revolutionary at the time, as they dealt with themes and ideas that were not considered fit subjects for literature. Shaw's genius was in being able to create characters and dialogue that captured the audience's attention and forced it to question accepted social and political ideas. In the award speech, Shaw's work was characterized by "his orthodox socialistic severity toward the community is combined with a great freedom from prejudice and a genuine psychological insight when he deals with the individual sinner." In the play *Major Barbara*, the lead character must make a choice between the spiritual efforts of the Salvation Army and the socialist philosophy of eradicating poverty as the most effective means of combating evil in the world. Other plays

George Bernard Shaw, whose satirical plays questioned accepted ideas, received the 1925 Prize in Literature.

In 1964, Jean-Paul Sartre received the Literature prize for the richness of his ideas, which had a far-reaching influence on his time.

confront the moral responsibility of those who profit from war, the eternal battle between the male and female view of the world, the class system and, always, the need for socialism as the basis of all economic and social systems.

At the height of the Great Depression in 1932, John Galsworthy was honored with the Nobel Prize in Literature, with special emphasis on *The Forsyte Saga*, a trilogy that explores the values of the capitalist society of the Victorian era. Like Shaw, Galsworthy creates complex and fascinating characters while showing us the eternal struggle between money and beauty. While the self-righteous assumptions of the ruling classes are exposed, the author's characters are all sympathetic and tragic in some ways and, like life itself, they are rarely simplistically all one thing or another, but a tragic mix of selfishness, longing, tradition and logic. Summing up the author's temperament with the word "gentleness," the Committee praised "that spirit of idealism, that warm sympathy and true humanity that radiate from all his writings."

Pearl Buck, one of the most popular novelists ever to receive the Nobel Prize in Literature, received her award in 1938. Born in China to missionary parents, she came to understand and love the land, culture and people of her adopted country. Her most famous work, *The Good Earth*, depicts a culture in which the ownership of land and the survival of the family are the most important things in the world. In making the award, the speaker said she opened "a faraway and foreign world to deeper human insight and sympathy within our Western sphere."

In 1947 the French writer André Gide was honored with the Nobel Prize in Literature. Gide's work, like so much other writing in the mid-20th century, was concerned with the problem of existence, the nature of good and evil and faith and morality in the modern age. Gide makes us confront the truth about ourselves and our world and the essence of our humanity. André Gide explored the problems of morality and religion in the 20th century with such honesty that the Nobel Committee put him

William Faulkner was awarded the 1949 Nobel Prize in Literature for his novels of life in the American South after the Civil War.

"in the first rank of the sowers of spiritual anxiety."

T. S. Eliot, one of the most popular and influential poets of his generation, received the Nobel Prize in Literature in 1948. His work is both difficult and popular at the same time. Born to an old and influential family in the United States, Eliot moved to London, England, as a young man and remained there for the rest of his life. Eliot's work confronted the challenge of maintaining traditional Christian values and faith in the modern world. The condition of modern civilization, as seen by Eliot, was characterized by its "aridity and impotence." His play *Murder in the Cathedral* about the 12th century murder of Thomas Becket has been performed on stage and also made into a popular movie. As part of the praise lavished on Eliot by the Nobel Committee, he was described as one of the successors of Dante and a poet whose work is "impressed with the stamp of strict responsibility and extraordinary self-discipline, remote from all emotional clichés,

concentrated entirely on essential things, stark, granitic, and unadorned, but from time to time illuminated by a sudden ray from the timeless space of miracles and revelations."

A year later, in 1949, the Nobel Prize in Literature was awarded to William Faulkner. His novels probe into the world of the American South in the years after the Civil War, when the bitter memories of defeat and the destruction of a plantation economy based on slavery created a special culture of remembered glory, and a distaste for the present. In this atmosphere, Faulkner captures, as a "probing psychologist," the way in which the human mind can create

Winston Churchill, a prolific writer in addition to being a famous politician, received the Nobel Prize in Literature in 1953 for his "mastery of historical and biographical description..."

Ernest Hemingway received the 1954 Literature prize for his powerful narrative prose in such classics as *A Farewell to Arms* and *The Old Man and the Sea.*

an atmosphere of evil and suffering. The Committee characterized Faulkner's ability to accurately and sympathetically portray this world full of bitterness: "he mourns for, and as a writer, exaggerates, a way of life which he himself, with his sense of justice and humanity, would never be able to stomach." The presentation speech ends with the description of Faulkner as "a great author who in a brilliant manner has enlarged man's knowledge of himself."

Winston Churchill, the British Prime Minister throughout World War II, was also a brilliant and prolific author. In 1953 he received the Nobel Prize in Literature. Churchill's literary works are many. Some cited in the presentation speech for special attention include *A History of the English Speaking Peoples, My Early Life* and *The World Crisis.* Churchill was so involved in the history of the first half of the 20th century, that his work comes alive in a way that is impossible unless you were there. As great as his deeds were, the Committee

noted that Churchill's words would inspire future generations long after his deeds are forgotten. The speaker concluded with what must be one of the most extraordinary lines of praise in Nobel history: "A literary prize is intended to cast luster over the author, but here it is the author who gives luster to the prize."

In 1954 the Nobel Prize in Literature was awarded to Ernest Hemingway, an American author who wrote in a uniquely

Albert Camus, philosopher and author of *L'Étranger* (The Stranger), received the 1957 Literature prize for exploring the problems of the human conscience through his writings.

Saul Bellow was given the 1976 Nobel Prize in Literature. His fiction analyzes contemporary culture not only realistically but also with optimism.

American style. Following in the footsteps of Mark Twain, Hemingway used direct and powerful narrative prose, to tell a story in the authentic language of the character. The combination of short sentences, vivid dialogue and action has made him a writer with a wide following. His two greatest novels — *A Farewell to Arms*, about his experiences in World War I, and *For Whom the Bell Tolls*, about the civil war in Spain, have become classics. Hemingway was a man for whom the fighting spirit came naturally. His fascination with war and the sea has marked him as a man of the new world, at home with risk and danger and anxious to carve out a place in the world against all odds. *The Old Man and the Sea*, a story about an old Cuban fisherman's battle with a huge fish in the Atlantic, is often cited as an example of Hemingway's belief that a man must physically engage with the world around him and fight for his dignity and his beliefs.

In 1958 the Nobel Prize in Literature was awarded to the great Russian novelist Boris Pasternak "for his notable achievement in both contemporary poetry and the field of the great Russian narrative tradition." His most famous work is undoubtedly *Doctor Zhivago*. When he learned of the award, he replied by telegram to the Nobel Committee that he was "immensely thankful, touched, proud, astonished, abashed." However, four days later, under pressure from the Soviet government, he rejected the award saying, "Considering the meaning this award has been given in the society to which I belong, I must reject this undeserved prize..." Although he was not allowed to accept the prize, the award remains as rightful acknowledgement of the accomplishments

William Golding, best known for his allegorical novel *The Lord of the Flies,* received the 1983 Literature prize for his insightful depictions of the human condition.

Aleksandr Solzhenitsyn, awarded the 1970 Literature prize, gave expression through his writing to the tragedy of the Russian lives that were sacrificed by the Soviet government.

of one of the great writers of our time and a legitimate heir in the grand tradition of Russian novelists.

The Nobel Prize in Literature for 1964 was awarded to the French intellectual Jean-Paul Sartre in recognition that his work "rich in ideas and filled with the spirit of freedom and the quest for truth, has exerted a far-reaching influence on our age." Because of his belief that, to retain his independence and perspective, a writer needs total independence and cannot be involved in any way with organizations of any kind, Sartre refused to accept the prize. In rejecting the award, he said, "a writer's accepting such an honor would be to associate his personal commitments with the awarding institution, and that, above all, a writer should not allow himself to be turned into an institution."

Samuel Beckett was awarded the Nobel Prize in Literature in 1969. His most famous work is the play *Waiting for Godot,* which exposes the meaninglessness of life about which Beckett felt so strongly. Like Sartre and many other post-war writers and philosophers, Beckett saw that traditional

assumptions about values and the meaning of life were no longer valid for many people. Yet, despite the emptiness of his characters' existence, Beckett's love of mankind, and his compassion for their suffering, redeem the bleakness of his drama and, in the end, his characters find the strength to endure in the companionship of others.

Aleksandr Solzhenitsyn received the Nobel Prize in Literature in 1970. He was born in Russia in 1918 and lived through the communist revolution and World War II. The experiences and feelings he chronicles are a record of things he personally

In 1997, Dario Fo received the Nobel Prize in Literature for his written works in which he treated serious topics satirically to expose wrongs in society.

Toni Morrison, author of *Song of Solomon* and other novels with epic themes, was awarded the 1993 Nobel Prize in Literature for her narrative style and exploration of the role of black people in America.

witnessed. The descriptions of pain and suffering in his books give meaning to the tragedy of millions whose lives were lost at a time when the individual was willingly sacrificed to the idea of a national will and a collective soul. Solzhenitsyn recorded the mistakes and the inhumanity of his time but also, as the Nobel Committee expressed it in awarding the prize, "the individual's indestructible dignity."

In 1983 the Nobel Prize in Literature was awarded to William Golding whose first novel, *Lord of the Flies*, has become a modern classic. Golding's experiences in World War II convinced him that man possesses a seemingly limitless ability to do evil as well as an ability to sacrifice everything for the good of others. In the presentation speech, he is called a "writer of myths" since his work deals with universal problems. In presenting the prize, the Nobel Committee said that Golding believes "man has two characteristics — the ability to murder is one, belief in God the other." And, since evil is an inherent part of man and not a result of social or environmental conditions, he believed we must always be on our guard and always struggle to be on the side of good. Knowing what man is capable of should sharpen our senses and alert us to danger so that the horrors of the past do not happen again.

Toni Morrison received the Nobel Prize in Literature in 1993. Her work is rooted in the American South and is concerned with the search for meaning and fulfillment, especially in the areas of sex, gender and race. Morrison looks back at her African heritage and the need to break free from a past composed of slavery and repression. Yet she also realizes the need for all people to create a past as well as a future for themselves in order to answer the most fundamental question: "Who am I?" Throughout her writings, no matter how serious the theme, humor, sympathy and warmth are combined with "a literary artist of the first rank."

Dario Fo received the 1997 Nobel Prize in Literature for his ability to create a "blend of

Doris Lessing received the 2007 Literature prize for her work in which she confronts social and political issues.

laughter and gravity [by opening] our eyes to abuses and injustices in society and also the wider historical perspective in which they can be placed." Fo is especially interested in exposing injustice in high places and is the voice of reason and the voice of the people in an age in which the complexity of modern life and the remoteness of government make us all feel helpless at times. Humor has proven to be one of the most effective ways of exposing injustice and folly throughout history and Fo has been called the jester of our time.

Doris Lessing, who received the Nobel Prize in Literature in 2007, was described by the Committee as one who "contributed to changing the way we see the world." Her large body of work explores woman's role in modern society and like a "hospitable earth mother" she is totally free of prejudice while being interested in the smallest detail of the average human life. The result is not only a very wide audience, but also an author who has been among the first to speak out on issues and injustices. Her life and her work have been an exploration of every woman's longing for love and freedom at the same time. In awarding the prize, the Committee said, "you have helped us cope with some of our time's important concerns and you have created a document for the future."

V.S. Naipaul was recognized in 2001 with the Literature prize for his storytelling, and his simplicity of language in describing the human condition.

The Nobel Prize

The struggle for peace during the 20th century has been long and difficult. World War I, the bitter years of the Depression, the rise of fascism in the 1930s and World War II left the continent of Europe and much of Asia in ruins.

The end of World War II in 1945 produced only an uneasy ceasefire between the two superpowers — the United States and the Soviet Union. The war of words and the arms race that characterized the Cold War exploded into fighting in Korea and Vietnam.

Against this dismal background, the Nobel Peace Prizes are a testament to the willingness of people from all nations to forge a peaceful solution to problems even in the most difficult times and against great odds. Perhaps the greatest victory for peace was the fact that throughout the second half of the century atomic war was averted, despite the creation and deployment of sufficient nuclear explosives to kill everyone on Earth many times over.

The Peace Prize has been awarded in three broad categories: individuals who have

Peace

worked in the political area and have made major advances for peace between nations; humanitarian organizations that have worked to overcome prejudice, repression and suffering; and individuals who have worked for human rights and justice in countries around the world.

Over the years, the Peace laureates have been men and women who have made an outstanding contribution to the creation of a better world. Some, like the four American presidents honored, have worked in the public eye. Some, like Mother Teresa, Albert Schweitzer and the Dalai Lama, worked long years in relative obscurity. Some, like Martin Luther King, Jr., Desmond Tutu and Nelson Mandela, have worked inside their own countries for racial equality and civil rights.

When presenting Barack Obama with the Peace Prize in 2009, the Nobel Committee reminded the world that the Peace Prize is much more than a recognition of past accomplishments. Its purpose is also to support and encourage actions that are essential in establishing a more peaceful and more just world.

Peace

In the struggle for world peace in the 20th century statesmen and world leaders have been recognized with the Nobel Peace Prize for their work in preventing or ending war between nations. Two American presidents were honored with the Peace Prize early in

American President Theodore Roosevelt was awarded the Peace Prize in 1906 for negotiating an end to the Russian-Japanese war of 1904–05. President Roosevelt used the award money as a "nucleus for a foundation to forward the cause of industrial peace."

the last century. Theodore Roosevelt received the prize in 1906 for his efforts to negotiate an end to the war between Russia and Japan. At that time, the United States was still only marginally involved in the affairs of other nations, and Roosevelt's efforts to mediate between two ancient empires was a major step in America's assumption of its place as peacemaker and world power.

In the same spirit, Woodrow Wilson was awarded the Peace Prize in 1919 for his work in drafting the 14 Points that formed the basis for the peace negotiations at the end of World War I, and which were fundamental in establishing the League of Nations. Although the world would be plunged into war again in only 20 years, Wilson's idealism and his recognition of the need for basic justice in dealings between nations, allowed the United States to play a key role at the peace table.

Following World War II, the Nobel Committee recognized an individual who had made an extraordinary contribution to winning the war and then in establishing the basis for peace in Europe in the difficult early years of the Cold War. In 1953 General

U.S. President Woodrow Wilson was awarded the Peace Prize in 1919 for drafting the 14 Points that formed the basis for the peace negotiations after World War I.

George Marshall received the Peace Prize for his work in rebuilding a Europe utterly devastated by war. Marshall began his life as a military cadet and rose quickly in rank and responsibility. During the war, he rose to become General of the Army in 1944, the highest-ranking soldier in the nation.

But it was not for his feats as a soldier that Marshall received the Nobel Prize — it was for his tireless work as Secretary of State in drafting and implementing the American program of post-war relief and reconstruction in Europe. Marshall was determined that the billions in aid dollars being poured into Europe would make a profound difference, rather than just temporarily relieving suffering. "Any assistance that this government may render in the future should provide a cure rather than a mere palliative," he stated. The success of the Marshall Plan, as the American assistance program was soon called, in assisting the European nations to rebuild is one of the great success stories of international cooperation. A man used to command, Marshall made the ideals of personal honor, self-discipline and self-sacrifice the watchwords of his life. At the time of the award of the Nobel Prize, Marshall was president of the Red Cross and continued his efforts to serve mankind.

American Secretary of State Henry Kissinger and Le Duc Tho representing North Vietnam spent four years negotiating a ceasefire in the Vietnam War, resulting in the Paris Peace Accords, for which they both shared the Peace Prize in 1973.

Willy Brandt, Federal Chancellor of Germany, spent his entire political life working toward creating a more peaceful Europe, and was rewarded for his efforts with the Peace Prize in 1971.

Willy Brandt received the Nobel Peace Prize in 1971 in recognition of his lifetime of work for peace in Europe. Brant was an early opponent of National Socialism in his native Germany and fled the country to live in Norway in 1933. From there he continued to write and speak against the policies of the Nazi regime. When Germany invaded Norway, Brandt escaped again, this time to Sweden, where he continued to write and speak out against Hitler. At the end of the war in 1945, Brandt returned to Berlin and became involved in the rebuilding of the city and German political organizations. During his tenure as Foreign Secretary of the Federal Republic of Germany, he worked to enlarge the European Community and to strengthen NATO. He also improved relations with the Soviet Union and Poland and reduced tensions between the countries by signing a non-aggression treaty with the Soviet Union and an agreement recognizing the post-war border between Poland and Germany. He was elected Chancellor of Germany in 1969. It is

for his "gesture of reconciliation across the borders of old enemies" that he was awarded the Peace Prize.

Henry Kissinger and Le Duc Tho were awarded the Nobel Peace Prize in 1973 in recognition of their four years' effort to negotiate a ceasefire in the war in Vietnam. The Committee recognized that a ceasefire was not peace or an end to the war, but was "a torch on the long and difficult road to peace." Kissinger, then Secretary of State, was unable to attend the award ceremonies, and Le Duc Tho refused to accept the prize because peace had not yet been achieved in Vietnam. In making the award, the Nobel Committee noted that not only was the end of the war in Vietnam an urgent matter, but that all nations must realize that "no one can assume the right to force his particular system on others by armed might."

The Nobel Peace Prize for 1978 was shared by Anwar al-Sadat, President of Egypt and Menachem Begin, Prime Minister of Israel for their efforts toward establishing peace in the Middle East. Both men had been deeply involved in the struggle to free their people from colonial rule after World War II. The ancient struggle between Jews and Arabs in the Middle East led to war between Israel and its Arab neighbors shortly after the formation of Israel in 1948.

Sadat's willingness to recognize Israel and go to Jerusalem in 1977 was commended,

Egyptian President Anwar al-Sadat and Israeli Prime Minister Menachem Begin were jointly awarded the Peace Prize in 1978 for their willingness to lay a foundation for future peace between their two countries.

as was the willingness of both men to meet at Camp David in the United States to lay "a foundation for future peace between these two one-time enemy countries." The Nobel Committee also had praise for the efforts of President Jimmy Carter, whom it acknowledged as critical to the success of the negotiations.

In 1994 the Nobel Peace Prize was divided between three men who had also worked for peace in the Middle East after decades of war. The recipients were Yasser Arafat, Shimon Peres and Yitzhak Rabin. Again, the Nobel Committee recognized that although peace still had not been achieved in the region, "our laureates have not only shown that a road to reconciliation can be found, but also very bravely taken several steps down that road."

Lech Walesa received the Nobel Peace Prize in 1983 for his leadership of the Polish trade union Solidarity. The Nobel Committee

especially noted Walesa's commitment to nonviolence and his determination to obtain the basic human right of working people to be able to negotiate the terms and conditions of their labor. His goal was simply the right to organize workers to negotiate for a better future. Walesa was commended for the "peaceful courage he showed when choosing his course." The Committee also noted the Polish Catholic Church's strong support of the nonviolent struggle had given Solidarity "invaluable moral strength." Although he had been released from prison before the award was announced, he did not feel that his position in Poland was secure enough for him to come to Oslo to receive the prize in person, a testament to how far the country still had to go in securing basic human rights for all its citizens.

Mikhail Gorbachev, President of the Soviet Union, received the Nobel Peace Prize in 1990 for "his manifold personal

contributions and his efforts on behalf of the Soviet Union" that made the dramatic improvement in American-Soviet relations possible. Gorbachev realized that the government in the Soviet Union, based on rigid central authority, had to change and he was determined to bring about that change. Largely as a result of his leadership, Poland, Hungary, Czechoslovakia and East Germany obtained their independence from Soviet control, and the arms race with the United States finally came to an end. It is not too much to say that Gorbachev's courage and realism brought an end to the bitterly divided post-war world. The Committee pointed out that, with Gorbachev, "confrontation has been replaced by cooperation." The Committee also referred to the Peace Prizes previously awarded to Andrei Sakharov in 1975 and Lech Walesa in 1983, pointing out that these two prizes had been received with "cool hostility" by the Soviet government at the time. Both Sakharov and Walesa were prevented from coming to Oslo to receive the prize and thus, Gorbachev's personal acceptance of the prize as President of the Soviet Union truly signaled the long-hoped-

for improvement in human rights inside the Soviet Union, as well as improved relations between nations.

The Nobel Peace Prize for 2000 was awarded to Kim Dae-jung "for his lifelong work for democracy and human rights in South Korea and East Asia." Kim Dae-jung was President of South Korea and, throughout his life, worked tirelessly for peace and the eventual reunification of North and South Korea. During the many years of military government in South Korea, he was imprisoned and faced considerable danger. Kim Dae-jung first ran for political office in 1950, but did not win a seat in the

Mikhail Gorbachev, President of the Soviet Union between 1990 and 1991, was presented with the 1990 Peace Prize "for his leading role in the peace process in the international community."

national assembly until 1961. He became President in 1998 when he ran as a reform candidate in a country that had suffered decades of repressive military rule. He had been an active supporter of those struggling for freedom in other countries, notably José Ramos-Horta in East Timor and Aung San Suu Kyi in Burma. The Nobel Prize Committee noted his willingness to break with the past and seek new ways to peace. To those critics of the award who said that peace and reunification in Korea had not yet been achieved, the Committee pointed out that the Peace Prize "is a reward for the steps that have been taken so far . . . It is intended . . . as an encouragement to advance still further along the long road to peace and reconciliation."

The Nobel Prize for Peace in 2009 was awarded to Barack Obama, President of the United States. The Committee, in its presentation, noted that he had moved the United States from a policy of confrontation to a policy of diplomacy, and that he envisioned a world free of nuclear weapons. To the criticism that his term in office had just begun, and he had not yet had time to successfully implement his vision for change, the Committee reminded the audience that "the Nobel Prize had not just been used to honor specific achievements, but also to give momentum to a set of causes. The Prize could thus represent 'a call to action'." The

Committee went further in explaining its reasons for giving Obama the prize so early in his term as president: "If the principles are important enough, however, and the struggle over them is vital to the future of the world, the Committee cannot wait until we are certain that the principles have won on all fronts. That would make the Prize a rather belated stamp of approval and not an instrument for peace in the world." Obama donated the approximately $1,400,000 US in prize money to charities that included the United Negro College Fund, the Hispanic Scholarship Fund, the Appalachian Leadership and Education Foundation and the American Indian College Fund.

U.S. President Barack Obama received the Peace Prize in 2009, and was encouraged by the Nobel Committee to continue his diplomatic work as "a call to action."

Human Rights

Albert Schweitzer was a brilliant student, theologian, organist and medical doctor. In 1904 he went to the French Congo to work with the Paris Missionary Society and began to dream of building a hospital in Africa. He initially raised funds for the hospital by giving concerts in Europe and continued his medical and humanitarian work in the Congo for the rest of his life. Schweitzer's philosophy is often expressed by the phrase "reverence for life," which summarized his belief that all human life has value and it is up to all of us to do what we can to help the less fortunate. His fame was so great that when he traveled to Oslo in 1954 to accept the Nobel Peace Prize, more than 20,000 people showed up to greet him. A spontaneous fundraiser resulted in donations to assist in his work that totaled more than twice the amount of the Nobel Prize.

Martin Luther King, Jr. received the Nobel Peace Prize in 1964. He was one of the most influential people involved in the great American Civil Rights Movement of the 1950s and 1960s. King was only 26 years old when he became the leader of the Montgomery, Alabama, bus boycott by black riders in 1955. The boycott was one of the first mass protests against the legal segregation of the races in the American South. A Baptist minister and the son of a Baptist minister, King fully believed that black Americans needed to follow the example of Gandhi and initiate a nonviolent

Albert Schweitzer, physician and humanitarian, received the 1952 prize for Peace.

Martin Luther King, Jr., a champion of civil rights and nonviolent protest, received the Peace Prize in 1964 for his message to the world that a struggle can be waged without violence.

struggle for their rights and to remember the biblical words of Jesus, "Love your enemies, bless them that curse you, and pray for them that despitefully use you."

After Montgomery, King won the respect and assistance of millions of Americans of all faiths and races through his refusal to accept the evil of discrimination or to condone the use of violence to achieve reform. At the conclusion of the presentation speech awarding him the Nobel Peace Prize, the speaker summed up King's impact on history: "He is the first person in the Western world to have shown us that a struggle can be waged without violence. He is the first to make the message of brotherly love a reality in the course of his struggle, and he has brought this message to all men, to all nations and races."

Norman Borlaug was awarded the Peace Prize in 1970 for his efforts to promote peace by increasing crop yields to ensure sufficient food for the poor. Often called the father of the "green revolution," Borlaug was a geneticist who created new strains of crops that vastly increased grain yields in Mexico, India and Pakistan. The Nobel Committee noted that Borlaug had helped fulfill the basic human right to have enough to eat, and that he had enabled the level of food production to increase to match the population explosion. In his Nobel lecture after receiving the prize, Borlaug pointed out that adequate food was a "moral right" of all mankind and that world peace could not be built on empty stomachs.

Andrei Sakharov, who received the Nobel Peace Prize in 1975, has been characterized

A Soviet physicist and human rights activist who also worked to end the arms race, Andrei Sakharov was awarded the Peace Prize in 1975.

as "one of the great champions of human rights in our age." Sakharov was a scientist who rose to prominence in the Soviet Union and worked on the development of atomic weapons beginning in 1948. He believed that the Soviet Union needed atomic weapons to maintain peace with the United States. In 1957 he began to feel a personal responsibility for the results of the radioactive contamination of Earth caused by nuclear testing. His efforts to end nuclear testing and the arms race encouraged others around the world. Sakharov founded the Committee for Human Rights to work inside the Soviet Union for human rights. In awarding the prize, the Nobel Committee noted that Sakharov had fought for peace "in a particularly effective manner and under highly difficult conditions." Sakharov was prevented by the Soviet government from traveling to Oslo to accept the award.

The 14th Dalai Lama of the Tibetan People, Tenzin Gyatso, was honored with the Nobel Peace Prize in 1989 in recognition of his insistence that the people of Tibet use only nonviolent means in their resistance to

the invasion and occupation of their country by China. Since 1959 the Dalai Lama and thousands of his followers have lived in exile in India, but he has remained a great influence for peace in Tibet and around the world.

A small nation of only six million people, Tibet could not stand against the military forces of China. As the Dalai Lama himself put it, his position of nonviolent resistance was the only option for Tibet: "In our case violence would be tantamount to suicide. For this reason, whether we like it or not, nonviolence is the only approach, and the right one." The speech honoring him with the Nobel Prize concluded with the words,

Tenzin Gyatso, the 14th Dalai Lama of Tibet, received the 1989 Peace Prize, in recognition of his insistence that his people use only nonviolent means in their resistance to the Chinese occupation of their country.

Mother Teresa received the prize for Peace in 1979 for her work with the Missionaries of Charity, a religious order that provides "wholehearted, free service to the very poorest."

"In awarding the Peace Prize to [His Holiness] the Dalai Lama we affirm our unstinting support for his work for peace, and for the unarmed masses on the march in many lands for liberty, peace and human dignity."

Mother Teresa, the founder and head of the Catholic religious order the Missionaries of Charity, worked among the poorest of the poor in India from 1948 until her death in 1997. At the time she received the Nobel Peace Prize in 1979, the Missionaries of Charity were working in over 20 countries and had directly helped millions of people. Her belief that in ministering to the poor, we are obeying Christ's commandments, and ministering to God himself is the driving force behind the order. Her work has been characterized by her total disregard for anything about a person other than their needs, and her recognition that the greatest disaster that can befall a person is to be abandoned and ignored by everyone around them.

Despite being a Catholic European woman working in India, she reached across all boundaries of gender, race, religion and language, and was recognized and welcomed wherever she went as an example of the best qualities of Christian charity. When she was awarded the Nobel Prize, she requested that the customary banquet given in her honor be cancelled. The Nobel Committee agreed with her wishes and donated the money to feed the poor. At her death, she was given a state funeral with highest honors by the Indian government. Mother Teresa was recognized not only for her work with the poor, but even more for her example of what can happen when people put their beliefs into practice and place the needs of others before their own.

The Nobel Peace Prize for 1984 was awarded to Bishop Desmond Tutu as one of the leading figures "in the campaign to solve South Africa's apartheid problem by peaceful means." His long years of nonviolent opposition to the brutal racial segregation laws in South Africa earned him respect around the world. His constant message to the black majority in South Africa was "Do not hate." Bishop Tutu became the first black general secretary of the South African Council of Churches and in that capacity made his influence felt throughout the country and around the world. He was especially active in his opposition to the deportation of more than three million black South Africans. Although racial discrimination was not confined to South Africa, perhaps nowhere else was it so much a

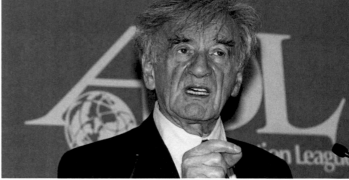

part of society and so intimately enshrined in the legal system.

Elie Wiesel received the Nobel Peace Prize in 1986 as a "witness for truth and justice" and "one of our most important spiritual leaders and guides." He was only 14 years old when he was deported as a Hungarian Jew to the Nazi death camp at Auschwitz, where his mother and younger sister were murdered. His father died while being transported to the death camp at Buchenwald. Wiesel survived the war and made it his mission in life to ensure that further atrocities of this kind were prevented by remembering the evil that was allowed to happen in the past: "We know that the unimaginable has happened. What

An Auschwitz survivor, Elie Wiesel was awarded the Peace Prize in 1986 for his efforts to eliminate evils such as genocide and nuclear war, and to ensure people do not forget the atrocities of World War II.

are we doing now to prevent it happening again?" His message is "do not forget" for if we forget, we risk a repetition of evil. Wiesel has supported the struggle for freedom in Latin America, Asia, Europe and South Africa and has worked tirelessly against the testing, spread and use of atomic weapons. He has

In 1984 Bishop Desmond Tutu received the Peace Prize for his nonviolent fight against South African apartheid. His message was "Do not hate."

remained a witness to evil who is not bitter or full of hate but, instead, full of the message that we must remain alert to evil in all its forms and make whatever personal sacrifice is necessary to prevent it happening again.

Aung San Suu Kyi received the Nobel Peace Prize in 1991 for promoting nonviolent opposition to the military regime in her native Burma. Her father, Aung San, had been a leader in Burma's struggle for liberation, first from British colonial rule and then from the Japanese invaders. The example of her father and Mahatma Gandhi inspired her wholehearted commitment to

Nelson Mandela, shown here, and Frederik de Klerk shared the 1993 Peace Prize, after they successfully and peacefully ended the South African apartheid regime and implemented a democratic government.

Aung San Suu Kyi helped to found the National League for Democracy in Burma, to peacefully oppose the ruling military regime. She was awarded the Peace Prize in 1991 for her "nonviolent struggle for democracy and human rights."

nonviolent resistance to oppression. She came to international prominence when the military government that held power in Burma refused to accept the results of a free election in which the National League for Democracy, a party she had been instrumental in founding, had won over 80 percent of the votes. Aung San Suu Kyi was placed under house arrest and could not attend the Nobel ceremonies, but her personal courage and persistence in the face of terror and repression called the world's attention to the situation in Burma.

The 1993 Nobel Peace Prize was awarded to Nelson Mandela and Frederik de Klerk for their efforts to bring about a peaceful end to the South African apartheid regime. When de Klerk became President of South Africa, he freed Nelson Mandela who had served 28 years in prison for his opposition to apartheid. On being awarded the prize, both men were congratulated for having the courage to break with the traditions of the past and to realize that South Africa

Carlos Belo, right, and José Ramos-Horta were awarded the Peace Prize in 1996 for their mediation, to find a "just and peaceful solution" to end Indonesia's violent occupation of East Timor.

had to establish a democratic government in which all its citizens, black as well as white, had equal rights and opportunities. In concluding the presentation, the two men were praised because their courageous actions had "given peace a chance" to bring about great changes in South Africa without great violence.

In 1996 the Nobel Peace Prize was awarded to Bishop Carlos Belo and José Ramos-Horta for their efforts to end the fighting in East Timor and achieve a just peace in the 20-year-old war with Indonesia. As a result of the occupation by Indonesia, as many as 700,000 people of East Timor are estimated to have died. This terrible slaughter has been called "the forgotten conflict" of our time because it has received relatively little publicity in the media. Throughout the fighting, Ramos-Horta offered mediation as

an alternative to more bloodshed and Bishop Belo supported the people's struggle for freedom and became a symbol of their hope for a better future.

The 2002 Nobel Peace Prize was awarded to Jimmy Carter, who was described by the Committee as "one of the most deserving and least controversial laureates for a long time." Jimmy Carter was President of the United States from 1977 to 1981 and was instrumental in restoring the nation's faith in its highest office after the resignation of Richard Nixon.

During his time as President, Carter arranged the Camp David Accords between Israel and Egypt. His deep Christian faith has

Former U.S. President Jimmy Carter was given the Peace Prize in 2002 for his efforts to find peaceful solutions to international conflicts and his work to advance democracy and human rights.

always inspired his work and he has, since leaving office, worked for peace and justice around the world. His humanitarian work has taken him to Haiti, Panama and Jamaica, and he has worked extensively for health and welfare concerns in Africa. His reputation for honesty has made him acceptable to all sides in overseeing elections in troubled spots around the world. During the presentation of the Nobel Prize he was described as "certainly the best ex-president the country ever had."

In 2003 Shirin Ebadi received the Nobel Peace Prize for her work to gain full civil and human rights for women and children in Iran. As a lawyer, judge, lecturer, author and activist, she is a powerful voice for justice in her own country and remains optimistic that peaceful solutions can be found to the differences that separate us. In awarding her the Nobel Prize, the Committee noted that her message of justice for all was important at any time, but especially at this time of great tension and change in the Muslim world. A woman of deep faith, she was especially pleased that the Pope was one of the first to congratulate her on her winning the Nobel Prize.

The Nobel Peace Prize was awarded to Wangari Maathai in 2004 for her lifetime of work for the environment, democracy and women's rights in Africa. A legend in Kenya, she was the first woman in her country to earn a doctorate degree and

the first female professor to teach at the University of Nairobi. As a biologist, she realized that the destruction of the forests of Kenya was causing widespread soil erosion and contributing to poverty and destitution among the people. Deciding to devote herself to work on behalf of the environment and the women of Kenya, she resigned from her teaching job. In 1977 Maathai began her campaign to replant the forests of Africa by planting nine trees in her own backyard. Since that time she has inspired poor women to plant over 30,000,000 trees in Kenya alone. A constant and tireless worker for women's rights and democracy, she has faced and overcome opposition all her life.

Barack Obama and Wangari Maathai plant a tree together in Kenya, in Nairobi's famous Uhuru Park. Maathai received the Peace Prize in 2004 for her work for the environment, democracy and women's rights.

Humanitarian Organizations

The Nobel Committee recognized the work of a humanitarian organization in 1901, the first year prizes were awarded. The Peace Prize was awarded to Henri Dunant who had founded the Red Cross in 1863 after personally witnessing the suffering of the wounded after the Battle of Solferino in Italy in 1859. Determined to do something to help, he insisted that the Red Cross should be permanently ready to assist the victims of war without delay. The Red Cross was the first in the world to realize that humanitarian groups should be formed in all countries and should work together in time of war or natural disaster. The Red Cross has become one of the most famous and highly regarded organizations in the world.

The Nobel Prize Committee has recognized the Red Cross, in addition to the initial award to Dunant, in 1917, 1944 and 1963. The first two awards were largely based on the efforts of the Red Cross during and after World Wars I and II to assist the prisoners and the sick and wounded on both sides. The award in 1963, the year that marked the centennial of the Red Cross, was

in recognition of its work with refugees in developing countries in Africa and Asia. The International Committee of the Red Cross, based in Geneva, shared the prize that year with the League of Red Cross Societies that includes societies from around the world.

In 1946 John Mott and the work of the Young Men's Christian Association (YMCA) was recognized for the work the YMCA had done for prisoners of war. In fact, the two great wars that dominated the 20th century were the background of many Nobel Peace Prizes in addition to those

In 1917, 1944 and 1963 the International Committee of the Red Cross was awarded the Peace Prize. The Red Cross objectives are to aid the sick and wounded in time of war and natural disaster.

The International Labour Organization (ILO) was given the prize for Peace in 1969. The ILO today is very active in the struggle against child labor throughout the world.

awarded to the YMCA and the Red Cross. Humanitarian work motivated by a spirit of Christian charity and aid to those in need was recognized with the Nobel Peace Prize awarded to the Quakers in 1947. The British Friends Service Council and the American Friends Service Committee shared the prize for their strong pacifist stand against any form of war and for their humanitarian work around the globe.

The International Labour Organization (ILO) received the Peace Prize in 1969 for its efforts on behalf of working people everywhere. The ILO has its roots in the 19th century labor movement in Europe and America. At the Peace Conference in Versailles in 1919 it worked for international recognition of the principle that the rights of working people were an integral component of a peaceful world. The ILO has been especially active in protecting children in the developing world who are exploited as a source of cheap labor.

In 1976, Betty Williams and Mairead Corrigan, the founders of the Northern Ireland Peace Movement, an organization that fought for the right of all people in Northern Ireland to live in peace without fear of violence received the prize for Peace. In making the award, the Nobel Committee noted that, unlike so many large organizations, this one has "sprung spontaneously from the individual's deep and firmly rooted conviction that the ordinary man and woman is capable of a meaningful contribution to peace."

In 1977 Amnesty International received the Peace Prize in recognition of its work to expose injustice and protect the human and civil rights of people around the world. Peter Benenson, an English lawyer, founded

Amnesty International in London in 1961 after he read about students in Portugal being imprisoned for making critical remarks about their government. Determined to help people who were imprisoned for nonviolent expression of their political or personal beliefs, he organized a movement to encourage a respect for human rights and to secure the release of people imprisoned for their opinions. The organization uses volunteers who appear in court to establish the right to freedom of thought, conscience, religion, opinion and speech.

Although its greatest weapon is exposure of the actions of repressive governments, Amnesty International feels that its greatest contribution to helping prisoners of conscience is to let them know that they have not been forgotten, that someone, somewhere is concerned with their fate and is actively working to obtain their release.

In 1985 International Physicians for the Prevention of Nuclear War, formed by American and Soviet physicians at the height of the Cold War, received the Peace Prize for its efforts to protest the spread of nuclear weapons among nations. In honoring the organization, the Nobel Committee pointed out that the organization has provided a "considerable service to mankind by spreading authoritative information and by creating an awareness of the catastrophic consequences of atomic warfare."

In 1999 Médecins Sans Frontières (MSF) was recognized for the efforts of its founder, Bernard Kouchner, and the doctors who gave their time and skills to work with people in need of immediate medical attention as victims of war and natural disaster. The organization's name [Doctors Without Borders] comes from its mission to assist anyone in need regardless of national boundaries or political beliefs. MSF is famous not only for its work in the field, but also for its willingness to create publicity to alert the world to acts of war against civilians and violations of civil rights. This belief that publicity helps to prevent acts of violence was highlighted when MSF representatives

The United Nations Peacekeeping Forces received the Peace Prize in 1988 for its role in helping the United Nations realize its peaceful aims.

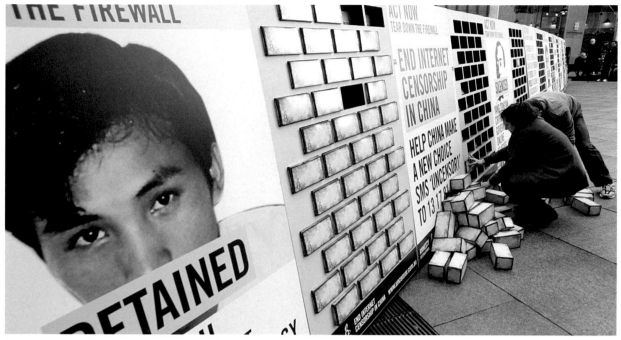

Amnesty International was recognized with the Peace Prize in 1977 for its work to obtain the release of those imprisoned for non-violent expression of their beliefs.

at the Nobel Prize awards wore shirts with slogans protesting the war in Chechnya rather than the traditional formal dress.

The United Nations has been the focus of world efforts to prevent war and obtain social justice since its formation in 1945. The work of the UN has been recognized many times as a forum where nations can come together to seek peaceful solutions to problems that in previous years might have led to armed conflict. The Peace Prize in 1954 and again in 1981 went to the Office of the United Nations High Commissioner for Refugees (UNHCR). The award in 1954 recognized the UN's efforts at humanitarian work and resettlement of refugees, primarily in Europe in the aftermath of World War II. By 1981 the problem of refugees had moved from Europe to Africa and Asia, especially the boat people

fleeing the war in Vietnam and refugees from Afghanistan and Ethiopia. The award of the Nobel Prize in 1981 focused world attention on the millions of people around the globe who were still homeless and often stateless. The prize money was used by the United Nations to establish a separate fund to help disabled refugees and 1981 was designated as the International Year of Disabled Persons.

The United Nations Children's Fund (UNICEF) received the Peace Prize in 1965 in recognition of its work in providing food and assistance to children and mothers in the aftermath of World War II, and for its efforts to better the lives of hundreds of millions of children living in poverty throughout the developing world by educating them about disease and nutrition. In 1959 the United Nations' Declaration of the Rights

Ralph Bunche received the Peace Prize in 1950 for his work with the United Nations especially in achieving a ceasefire in Palestine.

of the Child summarized the work and goals of the organization by stating that children everywhere in the world should be guaranteed protection from "all forms of neglect, cruelty and exploitation."

In 1988 the United Nations Peacekeeping Forces received the Nobel Peace Prize. Peacekeeping soldiers from United Nations member nations, wearing the distinctive blue UN helmets, are positioned between warring factions to prevent further bloodshed. The UN forces are only sent into a battle zone on the invitation of all the countries involved. At the time of the presentation in 1988, over 700 UN soldiers had been killed on peacekeeping missions.

On many occasions the Nobel Peace Prize has honored individuals whose life and work have been closely associated with the United Nations. In 1950 Ralph Bunche received the Peace Prize for his work as the

United Nations representative most closely associated with achieving a cease-fire in Palestine between the Arabs and the Jews over the establishment and survival of the State of Israel.

Dag Hammarskjöld was awarded the Nobel Peace Prize posthumously in 1961. He was Secretary-General of the United Nations and closely associated with the formation of the United Nations Peacekeeping Forces. He was honored for his work in resolving the Suez Crisis in 1956 and for his work for peace in the Middle East. Hammarskjöld was killed in a plane crash in 1961 while flying to the Congo to bring about an end to the civil war there, thus sacrificing his life in the service of peace.

Kofi Annan, Secretary-General of the UN, shared the 2001 Peace Prize with the United Nations. Mr. Annan was instrumental in reshaping the UN after the end of the Cold War.

For their work in publicizing the causes of global warming, Al Gore and the Intergovernmental Panel on Climate Change shared the Peace Prize in 2007.

Lester Pearson, a Canadian politician and future prime minister (1963–1968), worked actively for peace during his service at the United Nations, especially in resolving the Suez Crisis. He was awarded the Nobel Peace Prize in 1957 for "his personal qualities — the powerful initiative, strength, and perseverance he has displayed in attempting to prevent or limit war operations and to restore peace in situations where quick, tactful, and wise action has been necessary to prevent unrest from spreading and developing into a worldwide conflagration."

In 2001 Kofi Annan, Secretary-General of the United Nations, shared the Peace Prize with the United Nations. This prize, awarded on the 100th anniversary of the establishment of the Nobel Prize, was awarded to the UN for its efforts to make this a "better organized, more peaceful world." Kofi Annan, who became Secretary-General in 1997, was instrumental in reshaping the UN after the end of the Cold War and was involved in the fight against HIV/AIDS. In making the award, the Nobel Committee noted that this prize had two distinct functions, "both to honor the work that the UN and its Secretary-General Kofi Annan have already done, and to encourage them to go ahead along the road to a still-more forceful and dynamic United Nations."

In 2007 the Intergovernmental Panel on Climate Change (IPCC) shared the Peace Prize with Al Gore for their work on identifying and publicizing the factors causing global warming. This prize marked the recognition that work on behalf of the environment was now critical if we are to avoid disaster and suffering on an unprecedented scale. The IPCC is the United Nations panel charged with developing the science necessary to understand the atmospheric changes taking place. Their first report in 1990 was the basis for the Kyoto Protocol. Al Gore, a former vice-president of the United States, was cited as the single individual most closely identified with the issue of global warming, and the one who has done the most to prepare the ground for political change. He represented the United States at Kyoto, and through his books and lectures has continued to address the issue of global warming and the need to take difficult measures to halt the destruction of the atmosphere.

THE SVERIGES RIKSBANK PRIZE
IN MEMORY OF ALFRED NOBEL

In earlier ages, wealth was represented by tangible assets — land, gold, silver, jewels and physical possessions. Paper money as we know it did not come into widespread use until the 19th century and until the 1930s was usually backed by gold or silver. It was not until 1971, when the United States abandoned a fixed price of $35 for one ounce of gold, that the fixed relationship between paper money and precious metals was ended.

Today, the wealth of nations and the wealth of individual citizens are represented by numbers in a computer, and these numbers change in relative value to one another every day. Having money is no longer simple. Even the very wealthy can see the value of their investments wiped out overnight. And in the age of the credit card, all the purchase decisions we make are recorded electronically and privacy is becoming a thing of the past.

In this period of multinational corporations and national economies linked through international trade to an almost incomprehensible scale, the currencies and well being of people all over the world are

Economics

tied together as never before. Today, too, we have corporations that are wealthier than sovereign nations and investment banks that are so powerful they threaten to create a worldwide financial collapse if they get into difficulty.

The study of economics seeks to understand the way in which an economy works, how value is created, what happens when production and consumption patterns change, what happens when cheap labor causes production to move around the globe and what happens to nations that are not able to cope with rapidly fluctuating currencies and value. Economists also study what happens as populations age, how buying patterns change, and how savings rates are related to industrial growth and investment.

The role of the economist is to understand all these things and to educate and guide governments and individuals so that they can make wise choices. The men and women who are awarded this newest Nobel Prize have made an outstanding contribution in this field.

Economics

Ragnar Frisch and Jan Tinbergen were the first recipients of the Sveriges Riksbank Prize in Economic Sciences in 1969. Their pioneering work was devoted to creating mathematical models based on extensive statistical analysis that would allow economists to understand the workings of the economy in a precise way and to predict the effects of economic policy on the future. Their work formed the basis of modern economic thinking based on mathematical models.

The following year, in 1970, the prize in Economic Sciences was awarded to Paul Samuelson. He worked in four major areas of economics — how the economy behaves when it is outside equilibrium, the theory of how households relate their consumption of goods and services to income, questions

Paul Samuelson received the 1970 Nobel Prize in Economic Sciences for his ground-breaking research into how the modern economy works.

Milton Friedman, whose economic theory supporting free markets influenced many governments, received the Nobel Prize in Economic Sciences in 1976.

Robert Aumann shared the 2005 prize in Economics with Thomas Schelling for their research into how the principles of game theory apply to economics.

Franco Modigliani was awarded the 1985 prize in Economics for his analyses of consumption and saving patterns and how corporate valuation is determined.

of who actually benefits from international trade and basic work in capital theory that explains how much money is available and how it works in practice to create wealth.

Milton Friedman, one of the most influential economists of his time, was awarded the Nobel Prize in Economic Sciences in 1976. Friedman pioneered the study of the importance of the amount of money available in the economic system in determining the level of prices and wages. His most important book, *A Monetary History of the United States 1867–1960*, was especially influential in understanding the causes of the Great Depression.

In 1985 Franco Modigliani received the Nobel Prize in Economic Sciences for his work in understanding how households save and how corporations' market value is determined. His results are particularly significant in determining public policy in nations in which the percentage of older people is increasing rapidly. The Nobel Committee characterized his work by saying that it had "major significance to

research into consumption and saving." He also made significant contributions to the study of corporations and found that their market value was largely independent of their debts. This seeming contradiction provided the impetus for further research on how markets work, and what individual factors are most important in determining value.

Robert Aumann and Thomas Schelling shared the Nobel Prize in Economic Sciences in 2005 for their research into game theory and how it applies to the world of economics. Game theory attempts to understand why some individuals and groups are successful at cooperation and why some are in constant conflict. By understanding how groups interact over time, economists can predict how economic and social programs are likely to succeed or fail. Their work has been especially valuable in the analysis of trade policy and the long-term profitability of price wars and competition. The Nobel Committee noted that Aumann and Schelling shared a vision that "game theory had the potential to reshape the analysis of human interaction."

YEAR	PHYSICS	CHEMISTRY	MEDICINE	LITERATURE	PEACE
1901	Wilhelm Röntgen	Jacobus van't Hoff	Emil von Behring	Sully Prudhomme	Henry Dunant Frédéric Passy
1902	Hendrik Lorentz Pieter Zeeman	Emil Fischer	Ronald Ross	Theodor Mommsen	Élie Ducommun Albert Gobat
1903	Henri Becquerel Pierre Curie Marie Curie	Svante Arrhenius	Niels Finsen	Bjørnstjerne Bjørnson	Randal Cremer
1904	Lord Rayleigh	Sir William Ramsay	Ivan Pavlov	Frédéric Mistral José Echegaray	Institute of International Law
1905	Philipp Lenard	Adolf von Baeyer	Robert Koch	Henryk Sienkiewicz	Bertha von Suttner
1906	J.J. Thomson	Henri Moissan	Camillo Golgi Santiago Ramón y Cajal	Giosuè Carducci	Theodore Roosevelt
1907	Albert Michelson	Eduard Buchner	Alphonse Laveran	Rudyard Kipling	Ernesto Moneta Louis Renault
1908	Gabriel Lippmann	Ernest Rutherford	Ilya Mechnikov Paul Ehrlich	Rudolf Eucken	Klas Arnoldson Fredrik Bajer
1909	Guglielmo Marconi Karl Braun	Wilhelm Ostwald	Theodor Kocher	Selma Lagerlöf	Auguste Beernaert Paul d'Estournelles de Constant
1910	Johannes van der Waals	Otto Wallach	Albrecht Kossel	Paul Heyse	Permanent International Peace Bureau
1911	Wilhelm Wien	Marie Curie	Allvar Gullstrand	Maurice Maeterlinck	Tobias Asser Alfred Fried
1912	Gustaf Dalén	Victor Grignard Paul Sabatier	Alexis Carrel	Gerhart Hauptmann	Elihu Root
1913	Heike Kamerlingh Onnes	Alfred Werner	Charles Richet	Rabindranath Tagore	Henri La Fontaine
1914	Max von Laue	Theodore W. Richards	Robert Bárány	No prize awarded	No prize awarded
1915	William Bragg Lawrence Bragg	Richard Willstätter	No prize awarded	Romain Rolland	No prize awarded
1916	No prize awarded	No prize awarded	No prize awarded	Verner von Heidenstam	No prize awarded
1917	Charles Glover Barkla	No prize awarded	No prize awarded	Karl Gjellerup Henrik Pontoppidan	International Committee of the Red Cross
1918	Max Planck	Fritz Haber	No prize awarded	No prize awarded	No prize awarded
1919	Johannes Stark	No prize awarded	Jules Bordet	Carl Spitteler	Woodrow Wilson
1920	Charles Edouard Guillaume	Walther Nernst	August Krogh	Knut Hamsun	Léon Bourgeois
1921	Albert Einstein	Frederick Soddy	No prize awarded	Anatole France	Hjalmar Branting Christian Lange
1922	Niels Bohr	Francis W. Aston	Archibald V. Hill Otto Meyerhof	Jacinto Benavente	Fridtjof Nansen
1923	Robert A. Millikan	Fritz Pregl	Frederick G. Banting John Macleod	William Butler Yeats	No prize awarded

YEAR	PHYSICS	CHEMISTRY	MEDICINE	LITERATURE	PEACE
1924	Manne Siegbahn	No prize awarded	Willem Einthoven	Wladyslaw Reymont	No prize awarded
1925	James Franck Gustav Hertz	Richard Zsigmondy	No prize awarded	George Bernard Shaw	Sir Austen Chamberlain Charles G. Dawes
1926	Jean Baptiste Perrin	The Svedberge	Johannes Fibiger	Grazia Deledda	Aristide Briand Gustav Stresemann
1927	Arthur H. Compton C.T.R. Wilson	Heinrich Wieland	Julius Wagner-Jauregg	Henri Bergson	Ferdinand Buisson Ludwig Quidde
1928	Owen W. Richardson	Adolf Windaus	Charles Nicolle	Sigrid Undset	No prize awarded
1929	Louis de Broglie	Arthur Harden Hans von Euler-Chelpin	Christiaan Eijkman Sir Frederick Hopkins	Thomas Mann	Frank B. Kellogg
1930	Sir Venkata Raman	Hans Fischer	Karl Landsteiner	Sinclair Lewis	Nathan Söderblom
1931	No prize awarded	Carl Bosch Friedrich Bergius	Otto Warburg	Erik Axel Karlfeldt	Jane Addams Nicholas Murray Butler
1932	Werner Heisenberg	Irving Langmuir	Sir Charles Sherrington Edgar Adrian	John Galsworthy	No prize awarded
1933	Erwin Schrödinger Paul A.M. Dirac	No prize awarded	Thomas H. Morgan	Ivan Bunin	Sir Norman Angell
1934	No prize awarded	Harold C. Urey	George H. Whipple George R. Minot William P. Murphy	Luigi Pirandello	Arthur Henderson
1935	James Chadwick	Frédéric Joliot Irène Joliot-Curie	Hans Spemann	No prize awarded	Carl von Ossietzky
1936	Victor F. Hess Carl D. Anderson	Peter Debye	Sir Henry Dale Otto Loewi	Eugene O'Neill	Carlos Saavedra Lamas
1937	Clinton Davisson George Paget Thomson	Norman Haworth Paul Karrer	Albert Szent-Györgyi	Roger Martin du Gard	Robert Cecil
1938	Enrico Fermi	Richard Kuhn	Corneille Heymans	Pearl Buck	Nansen International Office for Refugees
1939	Ernest Lawrence	Adolf Butenandt Leopold Ruzicka	Gerhard Domagk	Frans Eemil Sillanpää	No prize awarded
1940	No prize awarded	No prize awarded	No prize awarded	No prize awarded	No prize awarded
1941	No prize awarded	No prize awarded	No prize awarded	No prize awarded	No prize awarded
1942	No prize awarded	No prize awarded	No prize awarded	No prize awarded	No prize awarded
1943	Otto Stern	George de Hevesy	Henrik Dam Edward A. Doisy	No prize awarded	No prize awarded
1944	Isidor Isaac Rabi	Otto Hahn	Joseph Erlanger Herbert S. Gasser	Johannes V. Jensen	International Committee of the Red Cross
1945	Wolfgang Pauli	Artturi Virtanen	Sir Alexander Fleming Ernst B. Chain Sir Howard Florey	Gabriela Mistral	Cordell Hull

YEAR	PHYSICS	CHEMISTRY	MEDICINE	LITERATURE	PEACE
1946	Percy W. Bridgman	James B. Sumner John H. Northrop Wendell M. Stanley	Hermann J. Muller	Hermann Hesse	Emily Greene Balch John R. Mott
1947	Edward V. Appleton	Sir Robert Robinson	Carl Cori Gerty Cori Bernardo Houssay	André Gide	Friends Service Council American Friends Service Committee
1948	Patrick M.S. Blackett	Arne Tiselius	Paul Müller	T.S. Eliot	No prize awarded
1949	Hideki Yukawa	William F. Glauque	Walter Hess Egas Moniz	William Faulkner	Lord Boyd Orr
1950	Cecil Powell	Otto Diels Kurt Alder	Edward C. Kendall Tadeus Reichstein Philip S. Hench	Bertrand Russell	Ralph Bunche
1951	John Cockcroft Ernest T. S. Walton	Edwin M. McMillan Glenn T. Seaborg	Max Theiler	Pär Lagerkvist	Léon Jouhaux
1952	Felix Bloch E.M. Purcell	Archer J.P. Martin Richard L.M. Synge	Selman A. Waksman	François Mauriac	Albert Schweitzer
1953	Frits Zernike	Hermann Staudinger	Hans Krebs Fritz Lipmann	Winston Churchill	George C. Marshall
1954	Max Born Walther Bothe	Linus Pauling	John F. Enders Thomas H. Weller Frederick C. Robbins	Ernest Hemingway	Office of the United Nations High Commissioner for Refugees
1955	Willis E. Lamb Polykarp Kusch	Vincent du Vigneaud	Hugo Theorell	Halldór Laxness	No prize awarded
1956	William B. Shockley John Bardeen Walter H. Brattain	Sir Cyril Hinshelwood Nikolay Semenov	André F. Cournand Werner Forssmann Dickinson W. Richards	Juan Ramón Jiménez	No prize awarded
1957	Chen Ning Yang Tsung-Dao Lee	Lord Todd	Daniel Bovet	Albert Camus	Lester Bowles Pearson
1958	Pavel A. Cherenkov Il 'ja M. Frank Igor Y. Tamm	Frederick Sanger	George Beadle Edward Tatum Joshua Lederberg	Boris Pasternak	Georges Pire
1959	Emilio Segrè Owen Chamberlain	Jaroslav Heyrovsky	Severo Ochoa Arthur Kornberg	Salvatore Quasimodo	Philip Noel-Baker
1960	Donald A. Glaser	Willard F. Libby	Sir Frank M. Burnet Peter Medawar	Saint-John Perse	Albert Lutuli
1961	Robert Hofstadter Rudolf Mössbauer	Melvin Calvin	Georg von Békésy	Ivo Andric	Dag Hammarskjöld
1962	Lev Landau	Max F. Perutz John C. Kendrew	Francis Crick James Watson Maurice Wilkins	John Steinbeck	Linus Pauling
1963	Eugene Wigner Maria Goeppert-Mayer J. Hans D. Jensen	Karl Ziegler Giulio Natta	Sir John Eccles Alan L. Hodgkin Andrew F. Huxley	Giorgos Seferis	International Committee of the Red Cross League of Red Cross Societies

YEAR	PHYSICS	CHEMISTRY	MEDICINE	LITERATURE	PEACE
1964	Charles H. Townes Nicolay G. Basov Aleksandr M. Prokhorov	Dorothy Crowfoot Hodgkin	Konrad Bloch Feodor Lynen	Jean-Paul Sartre	Martin Luther King Jr.
1965	Sin-Itiro Tomonaga Julian Schwinger Richard P. Feynman	Robert B. Woodward	François Jacob André Lwoff Jacques Monod	Mikhail Sholokhov	United Nations Children's Fund
1966	Alfred Kastier	Robert S. Mulliken	Peyton Rous Charles B. Huggins	Shmuel Agnon Nelly Sachs	No prize awarded
1967	Hans Bethe	Manfred Eigen Ronald G.W. Norrish George Porter	Ragnar Granit Haldan K. Hartline George Wald	Miguel Angel Asturias	No prize awarded
1968	Luis Alvarez	Lars Onsager	Robert W. Holley H. Gobind Khorana Marshall W. Nirenberg	Yasunari Kawabata	René Cassin
1969	Murray Gell-Mann	Derek Barton Odd Hassel	Max Delbrück Alfred D. Hershey Salvador E. Luria	Samuel Beckett	International Labour Organization
1970	Hannes Alfvén Louis Néel	Luis Leloir	Sir Bernard Katz Ulf von Euler Julius Axelrod	Alexandr Solzhenitsyn	Norman Borlaug
1971	Dennis Gabor	Gerhard Herzberg	Earl W. Sutherland, Jr.	Pablo Neruda	Willy Brandt
1972	John Bardeen Leon N. Cooper Robert Schrieffer	Christian Anfinsen Stanford Moore William H. Stein	Gerald M. Edelman Rodney R. Porter	Heinrich Böll	No prize awarded
1973	Leo Esaki Ivar Giaever Brian D. Josephson	Ernst Otto Fischer Geoffrey Wilkinson	Karl von Frisch Konrad Lorenz Nikolaas Tinbergen	Patrick White	Henry Kissinger Le Duc Tho
1974	Martin Ryle Antony Hewish	Paul J. Flory	Albert Claude Christian de Duve George E. Palade	Eyvind Johnson Harry Martinson	Seán MacBride Eisaku Sato
1975	Aage N. Bohr Ben R. Mottelson James Rainwater	John Cornforth Vladimir Prelog	David Baltimore Renato Dulbecco Howard M. Temin	Eugenio Montale	Andrei Sakharov
1976	Burton Richter Samuel C.C. Ting	William Lipscomb	Baruch S. Blumberg D. Carleton Gajdusek	Saul Bellow	Betty Williams Mairead Corrigan
1977	Philip W. Anderson Sir Nevill F. Mott John H. van Vleck	Ilya Prigogine	Roger Guillemin Andrew V. Schally Rosalyn Yalow	Vicente Aleixandre	Amnesty International
1978	Pyotr Kapitsa Arno Penzias R. Woodrow Wilson	Peter Mitchell	Werner Arber Daniel Nathans Hamilton O. Smith	Isaac Bashevis Singer	Anwar al-Sadat Menachem Begin
1979	Sheldon Glashow Abdus Salam Steven Weinberg	Herbert C. Brown Georg Wittig	Allan M. Cormack Godfrey N. Hounsfield	Odysseus Elytis	Mother Teresa

YEAR	PHYSICS	CHEMISTRY	MEDICINE	LITERATURE	PEACE
1980	James Cronin Val Fitch	Paul Berg Walter Gilbert Frederick Sanger	Baruj Benacerraf Jean Dausset George D. Snell	Czeslaw Milosz	Adolfo Pérez Esquivel
1981	Nicolaas Bloembergen Arthur L. Schawlow Kai M. Siegbahn	Kenichi Fukui Roald Hoffmann	Roger W. Sperry David H. Hubel Torsten N. Wiesel	Elias Canetti	Office of the United Nations High Commissioner for Refugees
1982	Kenneth G. Wilson	Aaron Klug	Sune K. Bergström Bengt I. Samuelsson John R. Vane	Gabriel García Márquez	Alva Myrdal Alfonso García Robles
1983	Subramanyan Chandrasekhar William A. Fowler	Henry Taube	Barbara McClintock	William Golding	Lech Walesa
1984	Carlo Rubbia Simon van der Meer	Bruce Merrifield	Niels K. Jerne Georges J. F. Köhler César Milstein	Jaroslav Seifert	Desmond Tutu
1985	Klaus von Klitzing	Herbert A. Hauptman Jerome Karle	Michael S. Brown Joseph L. Goldstein	Claude Simon	International Physicians for the Prevention of Nuclear War
1986	Ernst Ruska Gerd Binnig Heinrich Rohrer	Dudley R. Herschbach Yuan T. Lee John C. Polanyi	Stanley Cohen Rita Levi-Montalcini	Wole Soyinka	Elie Wiesel
1987	J. Georg Bednorz K. Alex Müller	Donald J. Cram Jean-Marie Lehn Charles J. Pedersen	Susumu Tonegawa	Joseph Brodsky	Oscar Arias Sánchez
1988	Leon M. Lederman Melvin Schwartz Jack Steinberger	Johann Deisenhofer Robert Huber Hartmut Michel	Sir James W. Black Gertrude B. Elion George H. Hitchings	Naguib Mahfouz	United Nations Peacekeeping Forces
1989	Norman F. Ramsey Hans G. Dehmelt Wolfgang Paul	Sidney Altman Thomas R. Cech	J. Michael Bishop Harold E. Varmus	Camilo José Cela	The 14th Dalai Lama
1990	Jerome I. Friedman Henry W. Kendall Richard E. Taylor	Elias James Corey	Joseph E. Murray E. Donnall Thomas	Octavio Paz	Mikhail Gorbachev
1991	Pierre-Gilles de Gennes	Richard R. Ernst	Erwin Neher Bert Sakmann	Nadine Gordimer	Aung San Suu Kyi
1992	Georges Charpak	Rudolph A. Marcus	Edmond H. Fischer Edwin G. Krebs	Derek Walcott	Rigoberta Menchú Tum
1993	Russell A. Hulse Jospeh H. Taylor Jr.	Kary B. Mullis Michael Smith	Richard J. Roberts Phillip A. Sharp	Toni Morrison	Nelson Mandela F.W. de Klerk
1994	Bertram N. Brockhouse Clifford G. Shull	George A. Olah	Alfred G. Gilman Martin Rodbell	Kenzaburo Oe	Yasser Arafat Shimon Peres Yitzhak Rabin

YEAR	PHYSICS	CHEMISTRY	MEDICINE	LITERATURE	PEACE
1995	Martin L. Perl Frederick Reines	Paul J. Crutzen Mario J. Molina F. Sherwood Rowland	Edward B. Lewis Christiane Nüsslein-Volhard Eric F. Wieschaus	Seamus Heaney	Joseph Rotblat Pugwash Conferences on Science and World Affairs
1996	David M. Lee Douglas D. Osheroff Robert C. Richardson	Robert F. Curl Jr. Sir Harold Kroto Richard E. Smalley	Peter C. Doherty Rolf M. Zinkernagel	Wislawa Szymborska	Carlos Filipe Ximenes Belo José Ramos-Horta
1997	Steven Chu Claude Cohen-Tannoudji William D. Phillips	Paul D. Boyer John E. Walker Jens C. Skou	Stanley B. Prusiner	Dario Fo	International Campaign to Ban Landmines Jody Williams
1998	Robert B. Laughlin Horst L. Störmer Daniel C. Tsui	Walter Kohn John Pople	Robert F. Furchgott Louis J. Ignarro Ferid Murad	José Saramago	John Hume David Trimble
1999	Gerardus 't Hooft Martinus J.G. Veltman	Ahmed Zewail	Günter Blobel	Günter Grass	Médecins Sans Frontières
2000	Zhores I. Alferov Herbert Kroemer Jack S. Kilby	Alan Heeger Alan G. MacDiarmid Hideki Shirakawa	Arvid Carlsson Paul Greengard Eric R. Kandel	Gao Xingjian	Kim Dae-jung
2001	Eric A. Cornell Wolfgang Ketterle Carl. E. Wieman	William S. Knowles Ryoji Noyori K. Barry Sharpless	Lelan H. Hartwell Tim Hunt Sir Paul Nurse	V.S. Naipaul	United Nations Kofi Annan
2002	Raymond Davis Jr. Masatoshi Koshiba Riccardo Giacconi	John B. Fenn Koichi Tanaka Kurt Wüthrich	Sydney Brenner H. Robert Horvitz John E. Sulston	Imre Kertész	Jimmy Carter
2003	Alexei A. Abrikosov Vitaly L. Ginzburg Anthony J. Leggett	Peter Agre Roderick MacKinnon	Paul C. Lauterbur Sir Peter Mansfield	J.M. Coetzee	Shirin Ebadi
2004	David J. Gross H. David Politzer Frank Wilczek	Aaron Ciechanover Avram Hershko Irwin Rose	Richard Axel Linda B. Buck	Elfriede Jelinek	Wangari Maathai
2005	Roy J. Glauber John L. Hall Theodor W. Hänsch	Yves Chauvin Robert H. Grubbs Richard R. Schrock	Barry J. Marshall J. Robin Warren	Harold Pinter	International Atomic Energy Agency Mohamed ElBaradei
2006	John C. Mather George F. Smoot	Roger D. Kornberg	Andrew Z. Fire Craig C. Mello	Orhan Pamuk	Muhammad Yunus Grameen Bank
2007	Albert Fert Peter Grünberg	Gerhard Ertl	Mario R. Capecchi Sir Martin J. Evans Oliver Smithies	Doris Lessing	Intergovernmental Panel on Climate Change Al Gore
2008	Yoichiro Nambu Makoto Kobayashi Toshihide Maskawa	Osamu Shimomura Martin Chalfie Roger Y. Tsien	Harald zur Hausen Françoise Barré-Sinoussi Luc Montagnier	Jean-Marie Gustave Le Clézio	Martti Ahtisaari
2009	Charles K. Kao Willard S. Boyle George E. Smith	Venkatraman Ramakrishnan Thomas A. Steitz Ada E. Yonath	Elizabeth H. Blackburn Carol W. Greider Jack W. Szostak	Herta Müller	Barack H. Obama

YEAR	ECONOMIC SCIENCES
1969	Ragnar Frisch, Jan Tinbergen
1970	Paul A. Samuelson
1971	Simon Kuznets
1972	John R. Hicks, Kenneth J. Arrow
1973	Wassily Leontief
1974	Gunnar Myrdal, Friedrich August von Hayek
1975	Leonid Vitaliyevich Kantorovich, Tjalling C. Koopmans
1976	Milton Friedman
1977	Bertil Ohlin, James E. Meade
1978	Herbert A. Simon
1979	Theodore W. Schultz, Sir Arthur Lewis
1980	Lawrence R. Klein
1981	James Tobin
1982	George J. Stigler
1983	Gerard Debreu
1984	Richard Stone
1985	Franco Modigliani
1986	James M. Buchanan Jr.
1987	Robert M. Solow
1988	Maurice Allais
1989	Trygve Haavelmo

YEAR	ECONOMIC SCIENCES
1990	Harry M. Markowitz, Merton H. Miller, William F. Sharpe
1991	Ronald H. Coase
1992	Gary S. Becker
1993	Robert W. Fogel, Douglass C. North
1994	John C. Harsanyi, John F. Nash Jr., Reinhard Selten
1995	Robert E. Lucas Jr.
1996	James A. Mirrlees, William Vickrey
1997	Robert C. Merton, Myron S. Scholes
1998	Amartya Sen
1999	Robert A. Mundell
2000	James J. Heckman, Daniel L. McFadden
2001	George A. Akerlof, A. Michael Spence, Joseph E. Stiglitz
2002	Daniel Kahneman, Vernon L. Smith
2003	Robert F. Engle III, Clive W.J. Granger
2004	Finn E. Kydland, Edward C. Prescott
2005	Robert J. Aumann, Thomas C. Schelling
2006	Edmund S. Phelps
2007	Leonid Hurwicz, Eric S. Maskin, Roger B. Myerson
2008	Paul Krugman
2009	Elinor Ostrom, Oliver E. Williamson

Credits

Index